What People Say...

"I often put books down after a few chapters because I was not captivated by the writing of our story. Not *The Angel and the Amazing Life of Maggie Love*. I had to turn the page to see what was coming next. I could visualize the characters, the streets, the rooms. I was on a power read until the end—and it took me just two days to read the book. I highly recommend you start reading this book."

—KF Avid book reader

"I couldn't wait to find out what happens next. This should be made into a movie."

—GS Bookkeeper

"*The Angel And the Amazing Life of Maggie Love* is a great story of love and conquering evil. I enjoy reading C.R. Fabis novels, his writing style is similar to Neal Shusterman and the main character Maggie Love makes me think of the Angela Constantine character from Terry Goodkind. C.R. Fabis' first book, *Rome Never Fell*, was a great story as well, blending two things I love to read: science fiction and history. I think C.R. Fabis is a great new author and hopefully has more good stories for us in the future!"

—SM Avid book reader

"C.B. Fabis' second novel, T*he Angel and the Amazing Life of Maggie Love*, offers a unique plot in the best tradition of the pulp-fiction genre. As a devoted reader of classic noir heroes like Kinsey Millhone, Phillip Marlowe, Sam Spade and others, Maggie Love has issues with injustice which results in inevitable reckoning. And so does the heavenly investigator who is assigned to get Maggie to justify her murderous actions to a heavenly panel of regulators.

"This novel is a real page turner. I especially enjoyed the short chapter style. I tend to have three or four books going at a time. I could lay this one down down and start right where I left off without having to re-read anything.

"*Maggie Love* reads like a Carl Hiassen story where the idiots, bad guys and their unfortunate decisions are brought to their attention. Maggie's form of justice is met out in often times creative but always ironic and unpredictable ways. This is a very good read, and I look forward to further books by C.R. Fabis".

—RM Avid book reader

"I LOVED this story. It was fun and engaging and had me always curious about the next thing we got to find out about her life. It's really a brilliant idea and loved how redemption is not always about what one thinks it is. I could totally see this as a TV series or movie!"

—CE Marketing Expert

"This is a great book. Gritty, well written. I highly recommend it."

—KW Realtor

"The *Angel and the Amazing Life of Maggie Love* is a masterpiece plot full of twists and turns. It leaves you entangled into the life of Maggie Love and wanting to read more. C.R. Fabis does an exquisite job bringing his characters to life, keeping you intrigued and entertained throughout. I look forward to reading more by C.R. Fabis!"

—KV

The ANGEL and the AMAZING LIFE of MAGGIE LOVE

C.R. Fabis

HUGO HOUSE PUBLISHERS, LTD.

©2024 Cal Fabos. All rights reserved.

No part of this book may be reproduced or transmitted in any form or by any means, electronic or mechanical, including photocopying, recording, or by an information storage and retrieval system without written permission of the publisher.

ISBN: 978-1-948261-73-9

Library of Congress Control Number: 2023920534

Cover Design and Interior Layout: Ronda Taylor, HeartworkCreative.com

Hugo House Publishers, Ltd.
Austin, TX • Denver, CO
www.HugoHousePublishers.com

To Maria

My loving daughter

who helped me

get through this ordeal.

1. THE ANGEL

MAGGIE LOVE IS FINALLY DEAD.

To be honest, I'm not at all sure about this assignment. The Consul gave it to me early so I could study up. This made me pause. She's a serial killer. Murdered twenty people. She has lived a horrible, mean life, and at first glance, she looks like the perfect psychopath. The thing I dislike the most is her smile. It looks fabricated. There appears to be no love in her and definitely no moral code. In fact, it appears that whenever she found a moral code, she did everything she could to break every rule the code tried to preach. Every law a country possessed—these seemed to be just rules for her to challenge. I'll give her that. She always loved a challenge.

Maybe that's why I was given this assignment. I needed a challenge. I needed to find out what was deep inside her. She really did commit perfect crimes, and she always did it with a twinkle in her eye and that charming smile on her face. Her acting skills were so good that she could have easily made it big in Hollywood. She didn't want that. She seemed to love the game of making people suffer, and when she was done with her work, her green eyes brightly sparkled. That seems odd to me.

She practiced her art with such a passion and with such perfection that she could not be caught. She did live well into her nineties and was never convicted of anything. There was only one time that Maggie made it to a trial, and that one was easy for her to manage.

I guess you could call me an Angel of sorts. Not like a Guardian Angel. No, those don't exist. We don't guard or guide you through anything. That is what you have to do with your own free will. What we do is inspect a person's soul. That is why we prefer to be called Inspectors simply because that is what we do, we inspect your souls.

THE ANGEL AND THE AMAZING LIFE OF MAGGIE LOVE

So now is the time for Maggie Love to pay the price for her sins. We have a long existing plan for this. She will commit these crimes all over again, but this time the result will be different and much worse for her. Each episode will end with pain, piercing her mind until it explodes. Again and again this will happen because I will make her relive different times of her life. They will never be in-sequence since time has no play here. Whenever her mind explodes, she will soon wake up in a different time. I will hopefully find something; even a small glimmer of repentance could be a sign. I know there is love in her somewhere. Hopefully. Maybe.

Fortunately, Maggie should never fully remember anything in the incidents, even that mind-blowing pain. I am not able to do this to a Being for eternity. That would be hell, and that's not our business. But if hell is her ending, that will be her choice.

My job is to find an ounce of good in her, and I have to admit, I need to find out why she did this. She doesn't seem to murder randomly. There must be something deep inside her soul, and I will do my best to find it. If I don't, she will be permanently terminated. That's real hell, by the way. This is the first time in a very, very long time that I'm not sure I can help a person save their soul. In fact, I have been serving as an Inspector for 2,646 years, and I have never lost a soul.

Losing Maggie would be a failure on my part, and failure is not acceptable on my watch.

1. In Her Fifties

MAGGIE WOKE UP.

She sat up in her bed as the room surrounding her was spinning like an insane merry-go-round. Around and around, at the speed of light, the room seemed to whirl. The pain in her head increased tenfold with the constant spinning. It felt like her mind had just exploded.

Slowly the rotation of the room began to slow. Maggie dizzily held her hands in front of her eyes seeing her very slightly wrinkled fingers. She got out of bed and was knocked to her knees as the room gave one last violent spin. Once up, she headed for a mirror over a dresser on the other side of the huge bedroom, and there she saw her face. There was a wrinkle here and there, but she thought she was still very pretty. Her dyed blond hair was muffled and messed up after a long night's sleep. Her green eyes still had a noticeable sparkle that stared back at her.

She hurried back to bed and picked up the new iPhone that was sitting on her nightstand. The date read November 4, 2007. Maggie was fifty-one years old. The memories were loading back into her head at an alarming pace. She recognized the penthouse condo she woke up in. She ran to a floor-to-ceiling window and was greeted by the morning sun. She saw patches of green flower-shaped trees with an oval of blue water in the middle. All this was surrounded by tall skyscrapers protecting the trees from the evil beyond. This was the New York City Central Park that she remembered.

"Why are you up so early, Anita?" said a scratchy voice from an old man sleeping next to her.

Maggie tried to remember who this man was.

With this memory failing she simply said, "Just enjoying the view, honey."

"Anita, we have been married for over six months now, and this is the latest you have ever slept in."

Anita? Maggie grabbed the small purse on the nightstand and searched it until she found an I.D. The picture looked like the reflection in the mirror, but the name printed on it was not Maggie Love. Instead it read, "Anita Hamilton Snell." A memory hit her in the head again and she suddenly became proud of that name; Anita Hamilton was her tenth alias so far. She quickly noticed that the birthdate on the license was the same as the date on the iPhone. Maggie put it together, "It's my birthday today, Clyde."

His name was Clyde. Clyde Snell, the seventy-eight-year-old billionaire real-estate tycoon. Maggie thought the little old man's unhealthy-looking white skin resembled that of an old white rhinoceros, with matching balding white hair to boot. She remembered his wrinkly old face hardly ever let out a smile.

He got out of bed. "Have the cook make some over-easy eggs with bacon and sausage."

They both put on matching black silk robes with black fur around the collars.

"Clyde, you know he likes to be called Chef Pierre, and he doubles as your nutritionist. Too much cholesterol in that breakfast he will say."

"I'm not in the mood, Anita. To me, he's a slop cook, and for what I'm paying him, he better make me what I want. And please get that haggy maid to bring us some coffee."

Maggie looked quickly around the bedroom trying hard to get all the memories back into her head. She felt that she had lived this day before. Her fake birthday was part of her well-thought-out master plan. She was thrilled she could live it again.

On the wall opposite the dresser, she saw what almost looked like a shrine. Maggie had designed this, and it was all as beautiful as she remembered. Three Japanese katana swords adorned the wall in front of a black darkly stained bookcase. The swords were varied in length with the largest on the bottom. Each one was held in its own wooden case or saya, lacquered in a shiny bright blue. The handles were dark yellow with four decorative red stars on each. She remembered the very expensive Asian figurines around the bookcase with fresh Asian flowers bringing in more color. Maggie took down the smallest sword and pulled it out of the saya revealing its razor-sharp steel blade.

I. THE ANGEL • 1. In Her Fifties

"Why are you so obsessed with those damn swords, Anita?"

"They're so beautiful, Clyde. They are more than a thousand years old."

"I know that, Anita. I paid for the damn things."

Maggie let her eyes shine at the old man. "Remember it's my birthday and you promised."

"Why do you want to ride on the subway? We have a chauffeur. I'll buy you anything you want, and I'll take you anywhere you want."

"You promised, and you know what I want. I want us to live one evening like regular people. You know it will be an adventure."

"Why I promised this I don't know; I'm too old for the subway. At least can we take the limo back?"

"Deal, and this will make you feel young again, Clyde. I am going to do some shopping after breakfast; then when I get back, we can start getting ready for our dinner date. Can you have the chauffer pick me up in two?"

"Yeah, yeah. I'll be glad when this night is over."

◦∞◦

Maggie had all the money she would ever need, and she planned to spend thousands today. She had already spent plenty on her unassuming get-away after the dinner date. Acting would come first, then she would magically disappear into the endless maze of the subway. She would be at the airport before 9:00 p.m. with plenty of time to catch her flight to Paris. The first-class ticket would be such a sweet trip to France. The passport she needed would be safely hidden inside her bra. Again, there would be no Maggie Love. The passport had the name Tommie Scott on the picture page. It was a perfect forgery of course, simply because Maggie had made it herself.

Maggie waited for the chauffeur to open her door in front of Bloomingdale's department store. She thanked him with a smile and told him to pick her up in three hours. Once inside the department store, she bought herself a yellow evening gown with a heavily padded top. This would easily hide the passport. Next came a long string of black pearls, a four-carat diamond bracelet, and a long black leather overcoat. For Clyde, she got a yellow tie to match her dress, a matching black overcoat, and a pair of brown dress shoes. She carefully inspected both soles of the shoes to make sure they were a little slippery. Maggie was positive that this was thirty thousand dollars well spent.

She had a store page take it all out to the limo and pack it in the trunk. Before she got in the limousine she was stopped by a handsome older man. "Can I talk to you for a minute?" he asked.

Maggie looked at the little graying man and thought, "Is this guy from this century or what?" He sported a long gray trench coat with a grey short-brimmed fedora on his head. His short, neatly trimmed beard matched his trench coat, and Maggie was at least a full three inches taller than he was. "I'm kind of in a hurry. What's this about?" Maggie asked.

"Mrs. Snell, I'm Inspector Lawrence. I just need to ask you a few questions."

"Do you have a badge or something, Inspector?"

"It's just a few questions," The Inspector said as he handed her a photograph.

"We've been looking for this woman for a long time. Her name is Maggie Love. Have you ever seen her?"

So far everything that was happening had a slight *déjà vu* in the back of her mind, but Maggie had absolutely no recollection of this Inspector guy.

"No, I don't know any Maggie Love. Never seen her before."

It was a picture of Maggie taken twenty-five years prior. She had shoulder-length brown hair and a pretty face that showed off the twinkle in her eyes. Maggie was sure her new disguise would hold up.

"We have good word that she is in this area. You'll let us know if you see her?"

"Sure, who do I let know?"

The Inspector handed her a card that read:
INSPECTOR LAWRENCE
CHIEF INSPECTOR TO THE CONSUL
999-999-9999

On the ride back to the condo, Maggie thought about the cute little Inspector. She thought he kind of resembled an angel from the 1940's. She also thought about calling the number with her iPhone. "What does Chief Inspector to the Consul do?" She thought as she decided against it. Her plan was too perfect to fail, and she was believing more and more every hour that it had already succeeded. Maggie threw the business card out of the limo's window because there was no way she would let that cute little man ruin her plans.

I. THE ANGEL • 1. In Her Fifties

As evening approached, Maggie got out of her shower. She had her own private bath with a four-person hot tub, a sauna, and a shower that rained down gallons of water from the ceiling above. She dried herself off with a fluffy red towel then looked at her nude body in a full-length mirror that was surrounded by gold leaves and flowers. Maggie was five-foot eleven-inches tall, and she definitely still looked sexy at fifty-one years young. Her legs were long and trim, her waist was tight and tanned, and she let her long blond hair gently hang over her shoulders. Maggie thought she would walk over to Clyde's bathroom to show him what he was missing. They had only had sex three times in six months and even that was three times too many for Maggie.

When Maggie walked into the bathroom, Clyde said, "Get your clothes on Anita. There's no time for hanky-panky. I want to get this night over with."

The slight rejection would make the evening a little more enjoyable for Maggie Love.

Maggie stood behind the shorter Clyde Snell and expertly tied a perfect Windsor knot in the yellow tie she'd bought. She smiled softly at him and said, "Perfect. You look so handsome, Clyde."

"If we're going to be like regular people, why do we have to get so dressed up?"

"Regular people get dressed up sometimes too." Maggie smiled and gave Clyde a soft hug. "We have a 7:00 p.m. reservation at the Momofuku Ssäm Bar, the best restaurant in the city."

"Why are we going there? I just want a steak," Clyde said.

"It's very close, so you won't be on the subway for very long, and they do have the best steak."

"You know, Anita, I'm not good at saying this stuff so bear with me. Out of my five wives, you have been the best. You have never given me any shit."

"I love you, Clyde. That's why I married you."

"I guess so. You signed that prenuptial agreement without a whimper. The others didn't do that without a big fuss."

"Oh, you're so silly. It's not about the money; it's about love. You treated those women so well, but they did not appreciate you Clyde."

"I did treat them well and a man has to put his wives in their place when needed. A man needs to smack them around when they get out of line. I especially did that to the second one."

"She deserved what she got. You didn't even get arrested when she died."

"Yep, I did her good. That's what money can buy you: cops and good lawyers. Look, Anita, you have been taking care of my wrinkly ass and my cranky old mouth, so here is a little something. Happy Birthday."

He handed her a rather large ring box.

"For me?" Maggie said as she opened the box. Inside was a brilliant six carat bluish-green pear-shaped diamond ring. The huge diamond was surrounded by another carat of sparkling white diamonds.

"You'd better not wear that on the subway. It cost two million. It is one of a kind."

"It's beautiful. I'll put it in my bag and put it on when we get to the restaurant. I want to show it off to everybody. I love you, Clyde," Maggie said as she hugged him tightly.

Clyde couldn't get himself to say it back, so he said, "So do I."

The "loving" couple took the short walk through Central Park to the Fifth Avenue subway station. They both wore matching long black overcoats to protect themselves from the cold New York night. Maggie accessorized with a large yellow-and-white handbag over her shoulders. She insisted that Clyde wear the yellow tie and the brown dress shoes she had bought for him. As they went down the stairs, Maggie escorted the older man carefully to the station. She looked for the N line north, and as they got to the platform, a giant silver train roared past them from the south, shaking the station with all its might. It slowed down then stopped with a long screech. The doors opened and people got off then people got back on. The Snell couple found two seats near the door.

Maggie took Clyde's arm and put her head on his shoulders. "This is so exciting," she whispered in his ear.

Soon a disheveled man in army fatigues with dirty brown hair and beard was standing in front of them. He had a small sign written by hand on a piece of cardboard. It read, "I will work for food."

"Get him out of here, Anita," Clyde said. "Give him some money. This guy smells bad."

Maggie reached into her bag and pulled out a one-hundred-dollar bill. "You can have this if you get out of here right now," she said to the man with a smile.

The homeless man grabbed the bill and ran to the other side of the train. He got off at the first stop.

"Four more stops and we're there. I told you this isn't so bad. We get off at the 14th Street Union Square station."

When they got to the third stop Maggie said, "Clyde, we have to get off here. I need to use the bathroom."

"Why? We're almost there."

"Come on honey, you know us ladies need to go more often than men."

Maggie made Clyde stand by picking him up by the arm. They quickly got off the train and Maggie made him wait on the platform.

"Just wait here a minute. I'll be back in a few."

"Well hurry up. Don't leave me alone for long in this god-forsaken place."

Maggie knew there was a train every four minutes. She would make him wait for two. When the first train passed, Maggie came back to join her husband.

"A train just left.'" Clyde said with frustration.

"There will be another one soon. Clyde, you know what we used to do when we were in high school? We would stand really close to the edge, then when the train goes by, it gives you such a glorious rush."

"No Anita, you're supposed to stay behind the line."

"Come on, let's try it. It will make us feel young again."

Maggie took his arm and used all her strength to pull a reluctant Clyde across the line. Clyde tried to pull back, but Maggie was too strong. She held him steady until the train was about fifty yards away.

As the sound of the approaching train started to fill the platform with a loud, long thunder, Maggie yelled in Clyde's ear, "Clyde! Do you remember Alison McLander?"

He tried to yell back, "What? Alison who? What are you talking about Anita?"

She had practiced the next maneuver hundreds of times. Maggie was always so well prepared. With a grimace on her face, Maggie swung to her right hitting Clyde in the back with the handbag hanging over her arm; then she nudged him with her right hip. This along with the slippery shoes worked to perfection. Clyde went falling into the pit with his arms and legs spread out, landing right in the middle of the track with a loud plop.

Maggie looked with delight as the roaring train smashed into him, cutting off his legs and arms and dragging the rest of his corpse ahead until the train stopped. Splashes of blood almost gushed their way to the platform above. As the thunderous train came to a stop, she got one of the biggest adrenaline rushes she had ever had.

Maggie could only enjoy the sight for a few seconds because now it was time to go into acting mode. She started to tear up and was preparing to scream hysterically about the death of her husband. Then everything got strange, nobody around seemed to notice what had just happened. People were still in a rush to get on and off the train but there were no screams and no crowd of lookers. And where were the police? The driver didn't even seem to notice as he sped on to his next stop.

When the train left, Maggie looked down at the blood and body parts below. She moved away and calmly waited for the next train.

Maggie got off the train at the 14th Street Union Square station.

She made her way to the rows of lockers she had visited two days before. She opened one with a key and removed a small black carry-on suitcase. Maggie pulled up the handle and rolled it to the restroom.

Once in a stall, she hung her overcoat on the hook and took off her dress. She took off her heels, nylons, and jewelry, and stuffed all of them into a brown paper bag. She replaced them with black denim pants and a red-and-yellow flowered blouse. She got into some yellow socks and pink sneakers and then came a tight wig cap. She put it over her head and forced her hair into it. Finally, Maggie removed a beautiful and expensive redhead wig out of the case. It was shoulder length and wavy, with big curls on the ends. She put it on and left the stall. At a mirror, she spent fifteen minutes adjusting her makeup. She reached into her bra and removed the passport and as Maggie compared the picture on the passport to the face in the mirror she said, "Perfect."

She added a pair of jet-black dark glasses, put on the overcoat and left the restroom. Anita Hamilton was now dead. She was survived by the much hipper Tommie Scott.

At ground level, Maggie threw the brown bag with the four-thousand-dollar dress and thousands more in jewelry into a trash can. She walked by a coatless old homeless man. He was holding out a tin cup, hoping some passersby would throw in some spare change. The sign hung around his neck read, "I will work for food." Maggie took off the coat and put it on the shivering man. Reaching into her bag, she took out the large ring case. She squeezed it into the tin cup.

"That's too much baggage to get into Paris," she thought. "I don't need the money anyway. That ring was perfect for Anita, but way too gaudy for Tommie."

Then Maggie hailed a cab.

―――

Maggie made it to La Guardia Airport. She already had her boarding pass and went through security with ease. Now all she needed to do was board the plane and enjoy her flight. This seemed too easy for her. No acting and no police. The ease of her task made her smile as she walked vigorously through the terminal. She suddenly felt a tap on her shoulder from behind. She turned around and saw the cute little Inspector man.

"You need to repent, Maggie. I need you to repent for the things you've done," he sternly said.

Maggie immediately went into acting mode. She took off her sunglasses and said, "Oh, Inspector! You startled me. I told you I don't know any Maggie Love. Maybe you can help me, I lost my poor old husband in the subway," Maggie started to tear up. "I am so worried"

"Maggie, I don't understand. If you lost him in the subway, why are you at the airport?"

Maggie said while starting to cry, "We were supposed to fly to Paris together. I thought he might have made his way here."

Maggie noticed a yellow handle above one of the buttons on the Inspector's trench coat. It had four decorative red stars.

"Maggie, why do you look so different? It is like you're in disguise. Maggie, if you repent, then this can be all over."

Maggie didn't repent. She thought fast. "I told you, I'm not this Maggie. I do not know who this Maggie is. Clyde and I love superheroes. We love Superman, so we were going to dress up. I am dressing like Lana Lang, and he was dressing like Clark Kent."

"I'm so sorry, Maggie. You still don't understand that you are dead."

The Inspector took one step back. With his right hand he pulled Maggie's large katana out of its bright-blue case. He held it firmly with both hands. With one mighty swing at Maggie, the shiny blade sliced off her head.

While her limp body fell to the ground, the Inspector calmly walked to Maggie's bodiless head. With the katana, he moved it, so her eyes were looking at her lifeless body.

Maggie didn't go into shock. She didn't "die" because that would have been redundant. She had to watch her quivering headless body as blood poured out of the neck. She had to feel the intense pain from every nerve she had. She had to gasp for air from a head that had no lungs. When the Inspector felt the time was right, Maggie's mind exploded.

II. THE ANGEL

The Consul was not too upset with my failure. They obviously didn't think this was going to be an easy job, and it was my first attempt at rescuing Maggie after all.

I know what you're asking, "What the hell is a Consul?" You think it's bad having one boss down on your world? Well, I have five. There are three female Beings and two male Beings that sit on the Consul here in the Bliss. That's what we call our world. A lot of people on the Below World (that's where you live), call it Heaven. Whatever you call it, it's a beautiful, serene place, and I have been serving the Consul since it was established and that was over five- thousand years ago. I knew that they would be very patient with Maggie, and the reason is simple. It is because she is a female soul. Since the Consul was founded, they have only terminated 206,504 souls. Of these terminated souls, only 306 were female. That is less than .2 percent. What was obvious here in the Bliss is way over the heads of the living bodies on the Below World. Maggie would certainly get a few more chances for me to find something that caused her to do this.

Why are we called Inspectors and not Angels? Like I said, it is because our main job is to inspect a surviving body's inner soul. Yes, the body is gone but that soul is still going. So deep inside we search, with the persistent hope that we will find a hint of good and some sound reason for the bad judgment and near insanity as a soul.

I work hard and with compassion, and I always hold out positive hope that I will be successful on every assignment. That is how I became Chief Inspector, and since I am Chief Inspector, I always get the most difficult assignments. Now that I've met her, I'm certain that this Maggie Love may be my biggest challenge ever.

Maggie is intelligent. She may be the smartest soul I've ever met. But she has a flaw. She is overly obsessed with perfection. She certainly isn't perfect, but she is delightful. Her physical beauty, even as she aged, reached far beyond any woman I had ever come in contact with. But she's an enigma; too evil and too wonderful at the same time. How could this be? She uses her beauty and intelligence to masquerade and murder. How could she perfect all that—and more?

The only conclusion I have at this time is that she was one of a kind. I've only met her once, and I can't wait to learn more.

2. In Her Twenties

MAGGIE WOKE UP.

The spin returned, gyrating so fast she couldn't make out a thing. All she could see was that the place she was in was way too bright; so bright that it warmed her skin. As she tried to focus on the light, her eyes squinted as the powerful beams of brightness temporarily blinded her. All this light surrounded her while the room whirled faster than a Category 5 hurricane.

It didn't take long for the spinning to subside, but the decrease in motion increased the pain in Maggie's head. It felt like her mind had just exploded, and in that moment, Maggie realized she was naked. There was a muscular, skinny man with short black curly hair and mustache on top of her moaning loudly. Memories started pouring back into her head, but they were not coming back fast enough. She felt penetration.

Maggie started screaming wildly, "Get off me. What the hell are you doing?" She started hitting the man with all her might to get him to stop. "You bastard, get off me!"

From a short distance away she heard a sharp raspy voice yell, "Cut!"

Now the spin slowed to a crawl and Maggie desperately looked around to try to get her bearings. Three bright spotlights were pointing at her. There were two big cameras on stands with a cameraman behind each. To her right, was another man holding a smaller camera.

"Sid, you moron! I told you to go easy on her today," the raspy voice said.

"I didn't do nothin' Boss. She just started freaking out," Sid replied with a heavy New York accent.

Gene Raymond was a tall balding man with stringy brown hair and mustache. His dark blue t-shirt barely covered his pot belly. Blood-shot beady eyes pointing out of his head clearly showed his anger.

Gene threw his clipboard on the floor. "Girls, make sure she's okay. I told you bitches not to use acid at work. Bring her to my office when she's come down from her trip." Then with all his anger, he roared, "That's a wrap for the day!"

Two young women dressed in white bath robes approached Maggie and helped her off the bed. As she stood up, they put a white bath robe around her. One last spin of the room made Maggie's knees collapse. The two girls held her up.

"Cilvia, are you okay? What happened? You were doing so good," a cute Asian girl asked.

A blond girl said, "Cilvia, there's some bad acid going around. You got to lay off that shit, Cilvia."

Maggie tried to absorb all the memories that were loading into her head. She looked at the Asian girl. It was Veronica. Veronica was her roommate.

"The boss wants to see you in his so-called office. I'd hate to be in your shoes," Veronica said.

The blond girl said, "Do you need more time, Cilvia?"

Maggie replied, "No, I'm good, and besides, I'm not wearing any shoes."

Maggie remembered where the office was. It was in the last bedroom in this four-bedroom rented house in the San Fernando Valley, California. Maggie confidently entered the room. As she entered, Gene quickly got up from a metal folding chair behind a dented and scratched metal desk.

He met her at the door as it closed and grabbed her tightly by both shoulders. "Do you know how much money that cost me?" Gene screamed in her face. "I'm trying to make art here, Cilvia. I can't make art without money."

He shook Maggie brutally back and forth. Then he slapped her hard across the face. He continued, "I told you whores, no drugs while we shoot." He slapped her again, then threw her on the floor. He looked down at her and pointed his finger, "I'd beat the shit out of you, but I need that face pretty. Now, get out of here, but do not leave. I want to talk to you and Sid later."

Maggie calmly got up. "I'm sorry, Gene. I didn't take any drugs. I just freaked out for a minute."

"Get out!" Gene barked back.

Maggie remembered where the girl's dressing room was. As she walked into the third bedroom from the back, the blond girl walked out, "Goodbye Cilvia, remember to stay away from bad LSD."

"Okay Sinister, I never touched the stuff."

Memories were flooding back every second. That's how she knew the blond girl was named Sinister.

Inside the room Veronica was getting dressed. The Korean girl was about two inches shorter than Maggie, and just as slender.

"How did you do in there?" She asked. "Gene was pretty pissed off."

"It was rough, but nothing I couldn't handle."

"Your face is red."

"You should worry about Gene, not me," Maggie replied.

Maggie saw a full-length mirror in the back of the room. She took off her robe and observed. Her body was near perfect. Her 35" bust wasn't just 35". They were perfectly round and natural. Her hips were the same measurement with a tiny skinny waist. She stepped back and noticed her body was tanned to a beautiful dark amber, no lines, just all tan. She had dyed her hair jet black. It was textbook straight and hung below her shoulders.

"Stop doing that Cilvia, you're making me hot," Veronica said.

Another memory went through Maggie's head. "I told you Veronica, stop coming on to me, girl."

"I know, but a girl can dream, can't she? I'm getting out of here. Are you coming home soon?"

"Soon, the boss man wants to talk to me. Veronica, what is the date?"

"It's Thursday."

"No, the date."

"February 10th, I think."

Maggie said impatiently, "The year?"

"You must have really found some bad stuff. Okay here it is, you are Cilvia Sky, that's Cilvia with a C. You are twenty-one years old, and the date is February 10, 1977. I'll see you at home."

⁓

Maggie and Sid sat in metal fold-up chairs across the metal desk from Gene. Maggie had changed into her street clothes while Sid was still in a white bathrobe.

"I'm sorry what happened earlier, Cilvia," Gene said with a little compassion. "But I'm the producer and director of this film. I have a responsibility to everyone on set. It's their livelihood."

"You haven't paid me in weeks," Maggie replied.

"I know that. See this script I have here?" Gene had a few brown pieces of paper with handwritten, barely readable manuscript scribbled on them. "This is going to change the adult entertainment industry. It is a breakthrough and people will line up around the block to see it. It will be bigger than *Deep Throat*."

"What's it called?" Maggie asked

"I call it *Cilvia Flies Sky-High*. I don't want your head to get too big Cilvia, but you're getting a little popular. It's written just for you. This script will require some serious acting."

Sid interrupted, "I'm into that Boss, I know I can act like Marlon Brando."

"Not you Sid. Cilvia. Your character is named Stupid Moron. All you have to do is play yourself. I just need your big dick."

"I'm up for that too, Boss."

"Shut up, Sid. I'm talking to Cilvia. You play a young woman that is trying to find her inner self through her sexuality. I have you in five scenes,"

"I'll think about it when you pay me the five grand you owe me," Maggie replied.

"Here's the deal," Gene made his beady eyes look bigger. "I'll give you ten thousand when the new film is complete. You must get better at this. I have you doing a couple of anal scenes and one double penetration."

Maggie stood up. "Gene, I told you I'm not doing that. What you got from me today is as far as I go."

"Then you don't get the ten grand."

"Fine, then I'll take my five and be on my way."

"Sorry, you don't get the five grand either unless you do the film."

"You're making a big mistake, Gene. You might want to reconsider."

Maggie started walking out of the room when Gene said, "We start production in two weeks. I'll give you one week to make up your mind. If you say no, no money and I will have a new film called *Sinister Flies Sky-High*.

Maggie walked out of the house and onto the front sidewalk. Another memory entered her head that she owned a car. She reached into her small bag and pulled out a set of keys. On one of them the VW logo was engraved, so she walked over to a red Volkswagen bug, opened the door, and got in. She knew how to drive but she didn't know where she was going. That would come to her soon enough.

One week was plenty of time to make up her mind. The déjà vu she felt while driving was overwhelming, and it told her that she already had made a decision. She already had a plan. In her head was the curious sensation that she had done this once before, and she was going to enjoy it all over again. The first thing she had to do was some fashion shopping. She wanted to create a totally new look.

While Maggie drove to her apartment, more memories came back to her. She pulled into the complex and parked her car in a parking space marked 321. With a shopping bag filled with clothes in her hand, she found an elevator and rode it up to the third floor. It opened to an indoor hall. She walked down the hall until she found a door numbered 321. She opened it with her key to find her home. Inside was a spacious living area with a good-sized kitchen to the right. Maggie remembered it had two bedrooms, and she also recalled that each girl had their own private bathroom.

Veronica came out of her bedroom. "Cilvia, how did it go with Gene?"

"The fat slob wants me to do a new film. He says it's written just for me. I'm not going to do it because he wants me to do things I don't do."

"You should think about it. This will be great for your career."

"Right. Why you so dressed up? Another one?"

Veronica had on a shiny, short leather dress and was wearing four-inch black heels. "You know it, I met a super-hot flight attendant yesterday."

"I'd give you a hundred bucks if I could be there when you tell your parents you're a lesbian."

"I might need you there for protection. I think they would like it better if they found out I was a porn star. Old Koreans don't agree with my lifestyle. They would kill me then dance at my funeral."

After Veronica left, Maggie went into her room, emptied the shopping bag onto her bed and found a pair of cotton, flowery red and yellow gloves with matching ankle socks. She put them on and spent the rest of the day with a bottle of Windex, cleaning everything in the apartment,. When she thought she was finished, she cleaned three more times. Now it was time for sleep. She definitely needed her rest. There was so much for Maggie to do tomorrow.

At nine the next morning, Maggie pulled the VW into the parking lot of a small strip mall in Reseda. She went into the biggest of the five businesses. Once inside, she slowly browsed through the merchandise. There were hot tubs of every size and shape, patio furniture, and lines of outdoor cookers. Then she came to what she was really interested in. A tall man with full-rimmed glasses and a pencil pack in the chest pocket of his white short-sleeve shirt approached her. "Welcome to Harvey's Outdoor World. I am Harvey himself; can I help you Ma'am?"

Maggie had on a brown conservative wig that was styled La Belle Époque with a wavy bun spun above her head. She wore a slightly nerdy navy-blue business suit, with black low-heel dress shoes. She also disguised her eyes with a pair of full-rimmed glasses.

She used her nasally, proper voice, "Yes, yes, you can. I have a client that is extremely interested in one of these. Do they have to go outside? Do you have free installation? Yes, yes, my client is extremely interested."

"If you have the space, we can install them anywhere. There is a very minimal installation charge, but it will be worth it. You cannot beat these for relaxation and a serene kind of therapy. I have thousands of satisfied customers."

"I see. I see that now. I need one with an extraordinarily strong door. My client does not want the heat to escape. How hot do they get? She wants it to fit three comfortably."

"Let me show you this model."

They walked down a row of wooden saunas and stopped at one with red cedarwood along the inside four walls and ceiling. The door had the only window, a two-and-a-half-foot square opening filled with a thick glass.

Harvey continued, "This is our most popular model. We call it *Sweet Sunset*. It's on special this week."

"I see. I see." Maggie looked through the window. It was set perfect for her height. "Like I said, my client wants the heat to stay in. Does this glass break?"

"It's plexiglass. I imagine you could break it if you hit it with a sledgehammer a few times. Not too many people do that."

"I see."

Maggie opened the door. Inside on the left was a wooden bench with room for two, facing a single bench. Next to the single bench by the door was a stainless-steel heater with a tray of about two dozen four-inch sauna rocks on top.

"How many times do I have to ask this?" Maggie tried to sound impatient. "How hot does it get? How hot?"

"I'm so sorry Ma'am. We recommend fifty-four to sixty-five Celsius. It can go as high as one hundred and ten if you pour water on the hot rocks. Some hard-core users can take five minutes at one-hundred and ten. Of course, we don't recommend that."

"Humm, that's 130 to 180 Fahrenheit and up to 230. Okay, I'll take this one."

"Good deal, Ma'am. Let us go to my desk."

As Maggie sat down, she handed the man a piece of paper. "This is my client's address. Her name is Veronica Kim. She's an up-and-coming Hollywood starlet."

"Okay, how are you going to pay, and when should we install?"

"Cash, and I need it installed on Thursday precisely at one o'clock. Veronica will be there. So, have your people be extra prompt and polite. You know how temperamental these Hollywood types are. Oh lord, I have to deal with this all the time."

"And your name, Ma'am?"

"Molly."

"Molly who?"

Maggie put on a pair of dark glasses and spoke almost entirely through her nose, "Ms. Molly. Any other questions?"

Maggie made it back to her car. "Only one more stop to go," she murmured as she headed for a 7-Eleven convenience store on Saticoy Street, a few miles away. This was a place she remembered all too well from her past. She parked in the back. At two in the afternoon, there wasn't much foot traffic behind the store. Maggie removed the business suit in the car. Underneath she had on an extra short pair of short shorts and a bare-backed red blouse. She kicked off her shoes and put on a pair of red high heels. The brown wig did not work. She threw it in the back and put on a short, blond curly hairpiece. While looking at herself in the rear-view mirror, she dotted her face with a cosmetic pencil, creating a few freckles. Now all she had to do was wait for her appointment.

Ten minutes later Maggie observed a woman wobbling from side-to-side as she walked, pushing a baby stroller. The middle-aged female had a green scarf covering all her hair. Her face was rough and scarred with patches of red blemishes and the carriage she pushed had a dirty red blanket covering where a baby would sit. The basket in the back was filled with empty aluminum cans and dirty rags. To anyone else this looked like a down-on-her-luck homeless person, but Maggie knew better.

She got out of the VW and approached the woman. "Hello Madam. You the lady I called?" Maggie was using her deep southern accent. "You got some of them goods for me?"

"Keep in down, lassie. You want to alert the entire L.A. Police force? You that friend of Maggie's?"

"Yeah well, can't say I'm a friend. Only met her two times, and I was so high on meth, I can't recollect what the hell she looks like. She did tell me if I ever needed anything to call Madam Gamora."

"Silence, lassie. No names here. I owe Maggie a few favors, so I got what you need."

"Thank ya. Let me see it."

"Where's the money, honey?" the sly Gamora asked.

Maggie reached into her purse and pulled out a wad of several hundred-dollar bills, "Here you go, sweetie pie." She handed her the cash.

"Don't give it to me," Gamora whispered intensely. "Give it to the baby."

Maggie reached under the red blanket and dropped the money into the stroller. Then Gamora reached in and pulled out a plastic baggie. Inside the bag were four smaller green baggies. As the older woman handed them over, Maggie could tell by the grain of the powder that this was some fine stash.

"This is some good blow, Madam. We are going to have a crazy fun party. What about the other stuff I asked for?"

Gamora reached in again and took out a white plastic unmarked twelve-ounce bottle. "This was hard to find. It will make your party guests so happy. They won't remember a thing, ever."

Maggie stuffed the merchandise into her purse, "Much obliged, Madam." She said as she hurried back to her car. As she drove away, she thought, "Shopping's done now. Just a few more calls to make, and the party is going head on."

―――

The next morning Maggie waited patiently for Veronica to get up. The young Asian beauty had a late night with her girlfriend, and Maggie knew today was a day off for her. Maggie looked relaxed in a light grey sweatshirt with a thick pink strip at her shoulders ending at a point near her waist. Her sweatpants matched.

At 11:00 a.m. Veronica emerged from her bedroom and Maggie said, "Good morning. You look like shit, Veronica."

"Never mix booze, coke, and dope. I just threw up."

"I don't plan on doing that. Veronica, I have a delivery coming today at one. Can you sign for it? It's paid for. I have some errands to run."

"Sure, I'm not doing anything today but recovering. What is it?"

"It's going to go right here." Maggie motioned to a clear part of the living room. "It might block the hall a little, but we will be okay."

"That's why you moved the couch, Cilvia? Okay I'll sign for whatever it is."

"Thanks, and you're going to love it." Maggie said as she left the apartment.

―――

Maggie spent the rest of the day jogging through the park. The Santa Ana winds that had been blowing intense and hard through the valley the past few days had calmed to a soft breeze. This left the San Fernando Valley smog free and a totally perfect seventy-two degrees. It was one of the few times she could enjoy the view of the majestic blue mountains to the north.

After jogging she had a late lunch making sure it was well past one when she made her first call. After 3:00 p.m., she found a pay phone. "Hello, Veronica?"

"I can't believe you bought a sauna. When can we try it?" Veronica asked. "Is it all set up?"

"Yes, the guys just left. Do you know why one of the guys would ask for my autograph? He thought I was a Hollywood star or something."

"Maybe he's into porn."

"He said it was for his daughter."

"Weird. Anyway, I'll be home in a jiffy. I have some exciting news to tell you."

"What news?"

"I'll tell you when I get there."

⁓

Maggie stood in the living room of her apartment studying her new toy. She checked the door and window to make sure they were sturdy and strong. A few modifications, and it would be perfect.

Veronica came in the room from behind. "It's so big, but it is so cool. It takes up half the living room. When can we try it?"

"Not for a day or two. I want to read up on it, so our first experience is perfect."

"What's this news you wanted to tell me?"

"Of course," Maggie looked at Veronica making sure her green eyes sparkled. "I've decided to do Gene's new film."

Veronica gave her a soft hug. "Great decision! This will do wonders for your career. Have you told Gene yet?"

"Not yet. I'm calling him later today. Veronica, I was thinking about inviting Gene and Sid over tomorrow night, to talk business and such. I'd appreciate it if you stayed away for the night."

"I have a date anyway. What time should I come back?"

"I should have them out of here around midnight."

"Cool, and Cilvia, what's with the matching gloves and socks you've been wearing, like all the time?"

"It's my new look. Do you like it? I'm going to ask Gene if I can use it in some of my scenes in the new film. This look, the sauna, it's all part of my plan to go all in with my career."

"When you go all in, you go all in," Veronica said with a smile.

⁓

Maggie stretched across the couch on her side with a green rotary phone, receiver over her ear. "Hello Gene. It's Cilvia."

"I hope this is good news Cilvia. I got fifteen till my next scene."

"I want to do the new film. I want to help you make the best adult film ever made."

"Great. I thought you would see it my way. We have production starting in a week and a half, and I will get you the address. This is a much bigger place Cilvia; I'm sparing no expense."

"Speaking of expense, I was wondering, could I get eleven thousand instead of ten?"

"No way Cilvia, I'm on a tight budget with this one."

"Okay, but I did hear that you were off on Saturday. Why don't you come by on Friday night? I have some of the best coke you have ever tried. We can talk business and such, and I need to show you something new I got. And oh, by the way, you should bring Sid."

"Maybe I'll show up for a few, but I certainly do not want to bring that idiot Sid."

"Oh, please bring Sid. We can practice some of the scenes you want me to do."

Maggie used a sexy singing voice, "I'll make it well worth your while."

"We will be there at nine."

⁂

Friday morning, Maggie sat at their kitchen table with that unlabeled twelve-ounce white bottle, and again waited for Veronica to get up.

As Veronica staggered into the kitchen, Maggie said, "How many times is the cat going to drag you in, Veronica?"

"I know. Cindy, the flight attendant, does not slow down. I feel so shitty bad. I'm having a tomato juice and vodka."

"You know that just prolongs the hangover. Veronica, I have three bottles of water in the fridge. Can you get them for me?"

Veronica opened the refrigerator and grabbed the three bottles. She put them on the table in front of Maggie. "Look at you with the matching gloves and socks again."

Maggie showed her the matching set. "Do you like these blue ones? I have twenty-two different styles."

"You're a nut. I just need some vodka."

Maggie took the white bottle and measured some of it into a tablespoon. She emptied the spoon into a measuring cup. She added one more spoon, then carefully poured the liquid into one of the water bottles. She started to repeat the process for the other two bottles.

"What are you doing now, Cilvia? You trying to be Ned the Science Guy?"

"No, I found this new energy drink concoction. It's all natural, just what I need to keep my energy at its highest for this new film."

"Can I try some? I need energy right now."

"No! Veronica, no. I'm not even sure if this stuff works. Let me try it on me, then I'll let you try it. You can smell it if you want."

Veronica picked up the white bottle and took a sniff. "Yuck, that stuff is gross. You drink it. It's better you the guinea pig than me."

"Perfect," Maggie said under her breath.

At 8:30 in the evening, Maggie was ready for her guests. She wore her grey and pink sweatshirt with a green pair of short shorts with matching green gloves and ankle socks. The cocaine was ready. She had four, three-inch lines complete with two straws waiting on the coffee table in front of the couch and in the kitchen was plenty of vodka and ice. The Chinese restaurant had just delivered fourteen containers of kung pao chicken, beef broccoli, and white rice just in case the men got the munchies. Maggie didn't think they would be here that long, but she wanted to be prepared just in case. At 9:15 p.m. the doorbell rang.

Maggie opened the door. "Welcome gentlemen. Come in." Maggie gave Gene a hard two-armed hug. Then she shook Sid's hand. "Sit down on the couch. We are going to have such a productive night. I have a few ideas for the film and as you can see, I found some of the finest blow on earth."

Before Maggie could finish her sentence, Sid had already snorted four lines of the stuff.

"Woo-hoo!" Sid yelled. His eyes were wide open and bloodshot with white powder around his nose. "This is some great shit, Cilvia. Where did you get it?"

"That's my secret. There is plenty for you too, Gene."

As Gene sat down to try the coke, Maggie went into the kitchen and returned with two highball glasses. "I got some of that Sky Vodka you like, Gene." She put the glasses on the table in front of the two men.

Gene ran the lines of cocaine through the straw and into his nose. "Wow, this is mighty fine."

"Nothing but the best for the best film maker ever," Maggie said.

"Hey Silvery, what's the deal with the gloves and socks?" Sid asked.

"My name is Cilvia, Sid. This is my new look. Do you like it, Gene? I thought I could use it in a couple of my scenes."

"I'll decide what you wear in your scenes. I prefer nothing, although it does look kind of hot."

Maggie walked over to the sauna and opened the door. She crossed her legs and leaned her body against it. "Did you see this?"

"Hey man. I know what that is. It's one of those things that you sit in that makes you hot and sweaty," Sid said.

"It called a sauna you moron," Gene said back.

Maggie smiled and let her eyes twinkle. "I thought maybe we could use it in the new film. It would make a great scene. Do you two want to try it?"

Sid said, "I do. I hear it's really good for makin' good therapy."

Gene shot down the entire glass of vodka. "Why would I want to get all sweaty tonight?"

"Once we get all sweaty, we can go to my room and practice some of the new scenes. It will be so hot, but first…" Maggie took off her sweatshirt and shorts. She stood there with only her green gloves and socks on. "You both have to get naked."

By the time Gene said, "I'll try it." Sid was already disrobed. Maggie held the door open as the two naked men entered. She instructed Gene to sit on the single bench while she sat next to Sid. She was closest to the door.

Gene sat down and said, "How hot is it in here? I'm sweating like a pig already."

"It's only 130 degrees. This will make it hotter." Maggie poured a glass of water over the hot sauna rocks.

"I'm getting some real good therapy shit," Sid said. He put his right hand on Maggie's breast.

She pushed his hand away, "Not yet, silly. We have to get all sweaty first." Maggie stood up. "Oh my gosh, I forgot the towels. I'll be right back."

Maggie opened the door and closed it behind her. She had finished those few modifications to the sauna. The generic door handle was replaced with a sturdy doorknob that had a key lock only on the outside handle. Then she found a big three-foot-long gate latch. That was attached just above the doorknob. She locked the door with the key, then placed the big iron bar securely into the latch. Maggie got out of the view of the window and turned the sauna up all the way to 180 degrees. She waited two minutes while listening through the wood.

She heard Gene say, "What's taking that bitch so long. How long does it take to get a few towels? My ass is burning up."

"Just open the door. Let some cool air in," Sid suggested.

Gene tried the door handle. "It seems to be locked."

"Let me look at it, Boss. I used to be good at picking locks back in New York."

"I know you're good at putting things in the hole, but there's no keyhole here, and besides, what are you going to pick it with, your cock?"

"Let me break it down then."

Maggie was out of their view with her hand over her mouth to try to stop from laughing.

She got a straight face and appeared in the window holding a few towels. She crossed her eyes slightly and used her dumb broad voice, "I got the towels, but I can't find the key. I think it is in my room. I'll be back in a jiffy."

Maggie got out of their view and listened.

Gene said, "This dumb cunt doesn't know what she's doing. Let's break down the door. Use one of those rocks to break the window."

Sid squeezed past Gene rubbing against his sweating belly. He picked up one of the rocks then dropped it, "Owwwie!" he screamed. "Damn it, Boss! That burned my hand bad."

"You're a dope, Sid. Of course, it's hot, we're in a sauna you moron."

"But you just told me to..."

"Shut up. Break down the door with your shoulder. I'm getting faint in here. My fat ass can't take this heat."

Sid started hitting the door with all his might. Using his shoulder, he pounded the door harder, but the iron latch still held.

Maggie's face appeared in the window again. "Sid, what are doing? Don't break my sauna, I just got it."

"Boss says his fat ass can't take this. We need to get out."

"I just remembered I left the key in my car. I'll get my robe and be back extra quick."

Maggie's face disappeared for a few seconds, then reappeared. "I'm so stupid. I forgot to tell you, there are some bottles of cold water in a cooler under the bench. Drink as much as you can because you must stay hydrated. I'll be back with the key in less than a half a jiffy."

Maggie ran to her bedroom door, then looked back through the sauna window. She saw the two naked men guzzling down the water. She abruptly turned around and slowly walked towards the sauna in their full view. Maggie stopped about two feet away making sure the men could see her. She crossed her arms over her bare breasts and gave them a Mona Lisa-like smile, making sure her green eyes sparkled through the window.

"Boss, this water tastes a little funny," Sid said with a yucky look on his face.

Gene looked through the window. "Why you standing there, bitch? Go get the key."

Maggie didn't say a thing.

The large dose of cyanide affected Sid first, burning his insides and cutting off his body's ability to breathe.

"I don't feel so good, boss. I think there's something in this water."

Sid started throwing up and shaking wildly. He fell into the tray of sauna rocks, knocking it over as he dropped to the floor, sending burning stones all over his dying body.

Gene started to feel the same thing. He heard Maggie say, "You roughed me up fairly good, didn't you? Remember Silvia, Silvia with a S, Gene. She loved the sky, Gene. She loved the sky."

Before he dropped, he stuck his face near the window. He looked at Maggie with his beady eyes almost touching the glass and tried to say, "I'm going to kill..."

He dropped to the floor and landed face down on top of the dead Sid.

Maggie unlocked the door and opened it to enjoy the sight of the messy, sweaty pile of dead men just for a few seconds. Then she locked the door and turned the sauna off. She sauntered into her room and changed into her long pink nighty. With her gloves and socks still on, she cleaned up the cocaine and went into the kitchen, emerging back out with a container of kung pao chicken and a pair of chop sticks. She sat cross-legged on the couch, liking her meal and waiting patiently for her roommate to return. Maggie was sure her theory of Veronica's habit of four dates would hold true again.

About an hour later, Veronica entered the apartment. She threw her purse on the floor and with teary eyes she said, "No more flight attendants. They're all full of it."

Maggie was still sitting at the couch. "Didn't work out? Such a big surprise."

"I'm not crying myself to sleep this time. Hell, with them. I'm thinking about switching to guys."

"That's the spirit. I've got plenty of Chinese and let me fix you a drink." Maggie tried to lift her spirits. "I've got some of Gene's favorite vodka." Maggie went into the kitchen.

"Great, how did it go with those guys?"

"So, so. Let's just say the project's been postponed for a while."

She came back with a highball full of vodka and handed it to Veronica. Veronica drank down three shots in one gulp."

"I'm quite surprised. Gene was so hot on that project."

Veronica held her throat tightly. She started to choke and went to her knees.

"Sorry girl. I really did like you," Maggie said as she looked into her eyes.

Coughing violently, Veronica could barely say, "Why?"

Maggie tried to explain, "You shouldn't have come on to me, but that's not really it. I couldn't resist the murder-suicide scenario." Maggie looked at the clock. "Oh my gosh, it's late. I've got a plane to catch."

As Veronica fell to her death, Maggie ran into her room. All her clothes were already laid out on her bed. She took off the nighty and stuffed it into an already packed suitcase. She sat on the bed to put on a pair of pantyhose. She continued to talk to Veronica, "You know there's enough in your diary to justify twenty suicides."

Maggie put on a sharp light-brown business suit with matching low-heel dress shoes. "Your fingerprints are everywhere and mine are nowhere. You even bought the sauna."

Then she stuffed her black hair under a tight wig cap. "I've got a redeye to Washington tonight. Washington D.C. that is."

She grabbed her dark brown La Belle Époque wig and went into her bathroom, "I have always been kind of into politics. Maybe I can find what I'm looking for there. I have uncovered some clues."

Looking in the mirror, Maggie placed a pair of contact lenses into her eyes, hiding the green and turning them dark brown. She put the wig on and took out a bright red tube of lipstick. Painting her lips vibrant red she said, "You know, I never liked Gene or Sid. They deserved what they got. You, I'm not so sure."

Back in her room, Maggie closed the suitcase and picked it up. Before she got to the front door she smiled. "Veronica, it's funny the way things work out. Gene's dead, Sid's dead, you are dead, and Cilvia Sky is now also dead. It's like The Beatles said, "Ob-La-Di, Ob-La-Da." Maggie put on the pair of full-rimmed glasses and used her most nasally voice, "Life goes on for Molly Jones."

～⚜～

Maggie loaded the suitcase into the front trunk of her car. She started it up and noticed she didn't have enough gas to get to LAX. A stop at the gas station on the corner was needed. She pulled next to a pump and reached into her purse for her wallet. It wasn't there. She searched again. No wallet. In frustration, she started up the VW and drove back to the apartment. She never made a mistake like this before. She planned everything too well. Even though there was plenty of time, the bodies would not be discovered for at least twenty-four hours. But still, she never made a mistake like this.

She opened the door to her former home and turned on the light. The bulb in the living room flickered on and off a few times like a strobe light, then it went dark. She thought she saw a little man in a grey trench coat and fedora hat standing in front of the sauna. He seemed to be trying to light a cigarette.

The Inspector flicked his lighter a few times until it ignited. "Hello Maggie." He took a deep drag on the cigarette. "I see why you people down here like these damn cancer sticks. They are so addicting and so good."

"Who the hell are you, and what are you doing in my apartment?" Maggie demanded.

The light suddenly came on and The Inspector handed her a card. "I think deep down, you know who I am."

Maggie looked at the card then flipped it back at the Inspector, hitting him in the cheek.

"Inspector of what? You'd better have a warrant, or you better get the hell out of here."

Maggie went into acting mode. "What happened to Veronica? Did you kill her? Please don't kill me."

"I didn't kill her Maggie. You did."

"She must have committed suicide. Things were going bad for her. And who is this Maggie you speak of?"

"Maggie, you committed the murders. Do you feel any remorse?"

"What are you talking about. I didn't do anything."

"And what about the two men in the sauna? What happened to them?"

Maggie held out her wrists as if to be cuffed. "If you want to arrest me, go ahead. Those men deserved what they got. You should see how they abuse us actresses. They beat us, they rape us, sometimes they even kill us. Believe me, they deserved it."

"That's true about the abuse, but they didn't deserve to die. This is not about arresting. It's about your eternity. What about Veronica? What did she do?"

"I didn't kill her. Veronica did this, all of it. She hated those guys. Wait a minute. You can't arrest me because there is no way you're a police officer. I'm getting out of here."

"You can leave, but I have this." The Inspector handed Maggie her wallet. "Just tell me, why Veronica?"

"I did like her, but this happens sometimes, she was just collateral damage."

"Collateral damage? Maggie, I know you want to see your masterwork one more time."

The Inspector opened the door to the sauna.

Maggie looked inside, then moved closer to see better. The bodies were gone.

"What happened to the...? I mean, it's just an empty sauna."

"Reach deep into your soul Maggie. Find the words to say you are sorry."

Maggie laughed, "You got nothin'. I'm out of here little man. See you later, gator."

The Inspector reached behind her and clutched her back. He pushed Maggie into the sauna, slamming the door behind her. He put the iron bar into the latch.

Maggie looked out the window. "Hey little Inspector man, let me out." She looked at the thermometer. It read 190 degrees Fahrenheit. "Okay, I repent. I'm so sorry, now let me out."

"Doesn't work that way, Maggie. It must be from your heart and soul. You can't repent just to save your ass."

Maggie knew she didn't have much time. She stripped down to her bra and panties. She took off the wig and cap. Laying down on the bench, she waited. After twenty minutes, the intense heat entered her body and brain until both were turning red.

She heard the Inspector say, "There's one bottle of water left in the cooler if you're interested."

Maggie could barely get up. She reached under the bench and pulled out the cooler. Opening it she looked at the bottle. She knew this would be much quicker than sweating to death, so she drank down almost the whole bottle and laid back down on the bench.

She didn't die. She couldn't. She did not black out. She just felt the pain. Red sores started to appear on her body, but the sores from the cyanide on her insides were burning her much worse.

The Inspector looked inside the window, observing the beautiful young girl rotting away. He felt something come out of his eye. "What is this? I'm crying?" He took a big drag on the cigarette and looked at his watch. It had been over twenty minutes. "Damn it. I'm being too easy on her."

Maggie's mind exploded.

III. THE ANGEL

There was a time when The Limbo was only a warehouse, or maybe more like a heavily controlled storage yard located just below the Bliss. The place was used only for souls that were waiting for their examinations to begin. While the soul waited in the Limbo, an Inspector would use the All-inclusive Records that were kept on every soul to recreate the time of their assigned souls' misdeeds. Since time was controlled in the Bliss, the wait was never too long.

Something happened in the year 1803, and the Limbo's main purpose had to be changed. The population of bodies on the Below World hit one billion. Chaos ensued because there were too many bodies and not enough souls. Growth continued at an astonishing pace, and now the Below World had over 7.2 billion bodies. Our only choice was to send souls back to the Below World for a second or sometimes third time. Some exceptionally good souls were being denied their graduation into the Bliss because of this.

At first, there was mass confusion in the Limbo. We started storing souls there that were going to be sent back to the Below World, and they were right beside the souls that were waiting for their examinations. A few mistakes were made. Our biggest blunder was made in the year 1889. We sent a soul that was waiting for examination back to the Below World by mistake. This soul would have surely been terminated. To the country of Germany he went, and his infamous name became Adolf Hitler.

Since then, we have been able to separate the Returners from the Waiters. Maggie's soul was now waiting comfortably in The Limbo. Fortunately, she's in what the Below World would call a trance, and so she is not aware of the examinations that I've been performing.

I will say that I was relieved when I felt something special in her soul during her last examination. I know it was ever so slight, but I knew it was something. It made me wonder why she could kill with such indifference. Why did there not seem to be any remorse from her at all?

I had to see what happened to her when she was younger. What set her off on this crooked path? I might need special permission from the Consul on this one. We usually never go back this far in a souls' life for an examination. At this age, a soul can't really comprehend the idea of repentance. The two male Beings on the Consul protested but the female Beings voted with me.

I needed to find out how a little kid named Maggie turned into Maggie Love.

3. In Her Ones

MAGGIE WOKE UP.

Everything was spinning. Maggie slipped off her feet and fell to the floor. She got up, and as the room started spinning faster, she fell again.

"Get up, Maggie!" she heard a female voice almost yell. "You can't be weak now. You have to use what I taught you."

Maggie tried to move closer to where the voice was coming from. She started to crawl.

"Maggie! Don't crawl like a baby. Get up!"

The spinning in the room started to subside. Maggie got up and looked at her little bare feet. The pain in her head was almost unbearable. She tried to be strong and started to walk towards a fuzzy image of a woman sitting in a chair nearby. She staggered as she walked, and the image of the woman started to come into focus.

"Mom?" Maggie asked as she got close.

Memories were coming back to her fast. She sensed that they were in some kind of a basement.

"How many times have I told you? Never call me that."

The woman was tall and slender, and her face was soft and pretty, but her nose did not seem right. It was slightly crooked, like it had been badly broken. Maggie remembered the brown hair that hung loosely over her shoulders.

She scowled at Maggie with her big green eyes. "We were working on your drills Maggie, and you suddenly fell down."

Maggie wanted to cry, but she stayed strong and said, "I don't know what happened, I just got so dizzy and fell. My head hurts so bad."

"Let's take a short break. I'll get you something to eat. I had them deliver some of that Chinese food you like."

"Yummy, did you get chopsticks?"

"Yes. Maggie, what's your last name?"

Maggie remembered, "I don't have one."

"Good, now what is my name?"

"Jane."

"Right, and what is that man's name that lives here?"

"Who, Dad?"

"No, Maggie. Never call him that."

"Oh yeah, I remember. His name is John." Maggie asked, "Jane, when's my birthday?"

"Maggie you're having a bad day. For a girl that reads at a college level, there is no excuse for this behavior. You know you don't have a birthday. You were born in a basement like this."

"Well then, how do you know how old I am?"

"After lunch, more drills for you. And you know that you are seven years old," Jane said, as she walked up the basement stairs.

Once alone, Maggie looked around the basement. There was a dollhouse, lots of stuffed animals scattered about, and a small single bed with a canopy over the top. There was an old TV and a record turntable. She remembered the bathroom and ran into it. In the mirror, she saw a kid with big green eyes and brown hair that looked like a miniature version of the woman that just went up the stairs.

Maggie went to the staircase and quietly walked up. She then remembered that she was not allowed upstairs. She also sensed that the phone would ring shortly. Once upstairs, she hid behind a couch and waited for Jane to pick up the phone. She listened intently.

"Hello, Rob?" Jane asked. "Again, Rob? They found us much faster this time, but I already knew that. What? You have another plan? They never work Rob. Your plans never work, and they will find us. We have to think about Maggie now."

She listened for a few seconds then said, "Okay Rob, you know we are always packed, and so is Maggie."

Alison McLander slammed down the phone. She noticed Maggie hiding behind the couch. "Let's go downstairs Maggie, fast."

Once in the basement, Alison picked Maggie up and sat her on the bed. She knelt in front of her and looked her in the eye. "We don't have much time. Listen and remember everything I tell you now."

"Is this another drill, Jane?"

"No Maggie and damn it, call me Mom." Alison's eyes started to fill with tears, "A long time ago, your Dad and I worked for some very bad people."

"You mean, John?"

"Yes, no, I mean he's your Dad. So, listen. He tried to steal money from these bad people, and he tried to threaten them with secrets he knew."

"Like a tattletale?"

"Yes. It did not work. The bad people want 'their' money—at least they think it's theirs—and they want to hurt us. We try to hide, but they always find us. That is why we have lived in so many different places, and that is why you were born in a basement. Nobody in this world except for your father and me even know you exist. If they did, the bad people would hurt you also."

Alison heard the basement door open upstairs. A tall dark-haired man in a business suit hurried down the stairs.

"I got the airplane tickets, so let's get out of here. We're going to Venezuela. We will be safe there," Rob McLander said. "What are you doing down here, Alison? We have to leave now."

"I don't like your plan, Rob. They will find us. It is all about Maggie now."

"It has always been about Maggie. Do you have a better plan?", Rob asked with frustration.

"I do, and I have been working on this for some time. My plan is already in motion." Alison stood up and reached into her purse. She pulled out her 38 Special Smith and Wesson revolver. She aimed it at Rob and fired once, striking him just above the right eye. His blood took a fraction of a second break before it spurted out of his head, then his shocked lifeless face fell to the ground.

"Mommy! Why did you kill Dad?" Maggie cried out.

"His name is John. Now listen. Forget about Alison and Rob McLander. Never think or say those names again. You have to be strong, Maggie, like we rehearsed." Alison tried to be stern with her daughter as she wiped away the tears.

"I don't care about McLander. It is just a name," Maggie said. She didn't cry.

"Listen please, Maggie. A young couple will arrive in a few minutes. They are your new mom and dad. They will be much more than foster parents. I spent a long time looking for them. Maggie, you're finally going to be able to go to school."

"I don't care about school Mom. I want to be with you."

Alison took out a white letter-sized envelope from her purse. From it, she removed a brass key, "Your bag is packed upstairs by the front door. Put this key and envelope in a safe place inside and guard it with your life."

"I don't care about keys. I want to be with you."

"Shut up and listen, Maggie. We do not have much time. When you are sixteen, take the key to the address on the note in the envelope. When you get there, a man will show you to a special kind of box. You will unlock the box with the key. Inside you will find everything you will ever need."

"I just need you, Mom. We can still get away."

Alison stood up. "Get up Maggie, the Hatfield couple will be here soon. From now on you are Maggie Hatfield. There is one more thing you have to do."

Alison handed Maggie the gun. "This is not a drill this time."

"Is it loaded?"

"Yes, do it like we practiced."

"I can't Mom. It will kill you."

"Do it Maggie. It will make you strong. When you are done, wipe the gun clean and leave it here."

"I will not. I can't. I need you, Mom."

"If you love me, you will do like we practiced. Now, Maggie!"

"No!"

"Now! I command you."

The déjà vu told Maggie she had no choice. She held the gun with two hands, aimed it at her mom, and pulled the trigger with two fingers. The bullet struck Alison in the middle of her forehead. Her green eyes lit up very brightly for a second, then they went blank. She fell to the floor in front of Maggie.

III. THE ANGEL • 3. In Her Ones

This time Maggie did not listen to her mom. She did not leave the gun. She confidently took it upstairs with the envelope and key. When she found the suitcase, she hid the gun and the envelope inside. Then, just as Alison predicted, the doorbell rang. Maggie opened the door.

"Hello, are you Margaret?"

"Yes. Well, I'm Maggie, and you two must be the Hatfield's," Maggie said dryly.

Maggie was trained very well. She hid her emotions deep inside of her.

"Why yes," said a blond-haired, big-eyed woman that looked to be in her twenties. She wore a red and white picnic dress that hung below her knees with a bright red bow in her hair.

She knelt down and gave Maggie a hug. "Look at her, Fred. Isn't she just gorgeous? She's the little girl I have always wanted. I'm Sally, but I want you to call me Mom right off the bat, Margaret."

"Okay Sally, I hate to seem pushy, but we need to get the hell out of here."

"Fred, isn't it cute how she talks like a grownup? Where is your Mom? I would like to meet her. We just talked and talked but always on the phone." Sally spoke in a southern country accent.

"Let's just say Mom is a little under the weather. Maybe you can meet another time. We have to go, now!" Maggie said as she grew more impatient.

"Okay, Margaret, what's the hurry? It looks like a little red splatter on your dress, is that blood?

Maggie responded, "Yes, I just got a bloody nose."

"Aww, does that happen often?" Sally asked with concern.

"No, this is the first time. We need to leave, like now!"

Sally tried to sound like the boss. "Fred, grab her suitcase and let's go."

He went in and took the case. Fred looked to be about ten years older than his wife. His short brown beard looked like a five-day old, five o'clock shadow. Under his blue denim overalls was the smell of sweat and beer.

They got into a brown rusty old 1952 Ford pickup truck. Maggie had to sit in the middle between them.

"Should be back at the farm in about an hour, if Ole' Bill can make it," Fred said with a thicker country accent than Sally's.

"Farm? Old Bill? What is he talking about, Sally?" Maggie asked.

"Ole' Bill is what he calls the truck. Sometimes I think he loves the truck more than he loves me." Sally answered.

"I think you're right Sally," Fred said with a yuk-yuk-yuk kind of laugh.

"Why does he smell so bad?" Maggie asked.

Sally answered, "He started drinking a little early today."

"Not true," Fred tried to defend. "That's what farm life smells like Little Missy. You'd better get used to it."

"Yes Margaret, we have a small farm a little east of Byers. We got chickens, four pigs, three cows and a horse. And yes, we have school. Your mom said you've never been."

"What's this Margaret stuff. My name is Maggie."

Sally said. "I will call you Maggie when you call me Mom."

A snowstorm had passed over the eastern plains two days earlier making the brown landscape turn into a soft white. Once they got off the I-70 interstate, it was slow-going. There was no snow removal in this part of town. The Ford truck had to barrel through about four inches of icy snow.

The farm they were heading to was located about sixty miles east of Denver, Colorado near the small town of Byers. It was a small two-bedroom farmhouse with an old-style kitchen and a wood-burning stove. Their new electricity had just arrived last year, and Hatfield's had installed a few electric lights around the house. Some of them were just bulbs hanging from the ceiling. There was a red barn in dire need of paint, and in front of the barn was a poultry- wired chicken coop with ten or so clucking birds inside. There was plenty of open land to plant a prosperous bounty of crops.

As they pulled the old brown truck onto a snowy dirt driveway in front of the house, Sally said, "This is your new home, Margaret. I have your room all ready."

Maggie said sarcastically, "This is nice. Which one's the house?"

"It's the brown one," Sally answered. "That red thing is the stinky old barn."

"The snow looks nice. I've been kind of cooped up the last few years. I think I could get used to this."

"You'd better Little Missy. Soon, I'm puttin' you to work," Fred said.

They entered the house and Sally showed Maggie to her room. There was a small living room and kitchen in the middle of the house with one bedroom on each side of the living area.

Maggie's room was the one on the left. Sally opened the door.

"This is your room. I fixed it up a little. Do you like it?"

The room had a small double bed with a red bedspread. There was an old oak dresser with a vanity mirror above.

"It's okay, but where's the TV and record player? I also need books. You might want to get a bookcase."

"We can't afford any bookcase. I had to use some secret money just to get the bed. Get some rest Maggie because we have an early appointment at your new school with the principal lady. I think they are going to let you start soon."

"That will be different. Did you know I never met another kid before?"

"Now Margaret, don't make up stories. It is not nice to fib."

"Not fibbing. Did you know I shot my Mom? Right in the head."

"Stop that. You sure have a wild imagination. Now put your things in the dresser, then after dinner, it's your bedtime. I'm making pork chops tonight."

"Can I have Chinese? It's my favorite."

"Nope. You're going to love my country cooking. My pork chops are to die for."

Maggie was tired. She had a big day. Alone in her bed, she tried her best not to cry. She could see her mom clearly inside her head. Her mom was always teaching her. She seemed to know everything, and Maggie loved that she passed it all on to her. The little girl tried not to think about the look on her mother's face when she pulled the trigger. Sleep was the best medicine now. As Maggie started to doze off, her slumber was interrupted by an argument coming from the kitchen area. It started softly, then it got louder and more rambunctious. She heard what sounded like dishes breaking. She covered her ears and went to sleep.

⚜

"I'm Principal Miner," said a stout woman in her later middle age as she sat down behind her large desk.

"I'm Sally Hatfield, and this is my foster daughter, Margaret. We are anxious for her to start school as soon as possible."

Sally handed the principal a stack of papers. Mrs. Miner put on a pair of thin-rimmed reading glasses and started to look them over. "Says here her parents are a Jane and John Doeskin. They give you full custody."

Sally said, "Her Mom was the dearest and they both loved Margaret so much. They have some issues to work out."

Maggie broke in. "They're a little under the weather."

"The name is Maggie on the birth certificate. So, which one is it? Margaret or Maggie?" asked the Principal.

They responded at the same time. Sally said, "Margaret" while Maggie said, "Maggie"

Mrs. Miner replied, "I guess it doesn't matter. It's just a name. We must give Maggie a placement test. Because of her early birthday, she should be in the third grade. Welcome to Byer's Elementary, Maggie Margaret."

Sally said with a little nervousness, "I want to tell you, she has never been to school before. Her Momma home taught her."

"I've been cooped up in a basement," Maggie said.

"Okay. You are such a pretty little girl, Maggie. I'm sure you will fit in just fine." The principal continued, "You can wait in the lobby Mrs. Hatfield. The test should take about thirty minutes."

About three hours later, the Principal had Sally come back into her office.

"Maggie is waiting in the other room. I need to talk to you alone," the principal said. "Mrs. Hatfield. It would be a waste of time for Margaret to go to this school."

Sally responded quickly, "I know she's never been to school, but she's my little girl now, and she deserves a chance."

"No, you don't understand. She is not fit for this school."

"Poppycock!" Sally stood up. "If she failed your little test, you should put her back a grade. I'm okay with that."

"Sit down, Mrs. Hatfield. You still do not understand. Maggie is a prodigy."

"She's a prodi-what?"

"We gave her the elementary exam, and she finished in three minutes. She got 100 percent. We gave her the junior high test and that one took two and a half minutes. Again 100 percent. She aced the high school test in just ten minutes."

"So, she's smart?"

"Your foster daughter is very special. I've never seen anything like this in forty-two years of working in education. She reads at a college level, maybe even more. She can remember everything. It seems she has some kind of photographic memory. Math seems to be her specialty. She understands algebra and calculus."

"I don't even know what that is. What am I supposed to do?"

"I'll call you. I am going to get in touch with some educators at the University of Colorado. We need some guidance."

Driving the old brown truck home Sally said to Maggie, "So, they say you are some kind of smarty-pants, Margaret. You don't have to go to that school. We should celebrate. I'm going to make you a special dinner."

"Chinese? please Sally."

"Nope, barbequed pork loin."

"Is pig all we eat around here?"

"We just killed one. We have to eat it."

"If I didn't love Chinese food so much, I'd turn vegetarian," Maggie said.

Maggie spent the afternoon checking out her new home. Being outside during the day was something she was not used to. Her parents would take her out occasionally to a restaurant or shop, but only under the cover of darkness. Now she was outside under the Colorado winter sun. There were patches of snow around the house and barn, and as she looked out to the east, she witnessed barren fields covered in a blanket of white melting snow under the bright sun at 5, 210 feet above sea level. A big round thermometer on the barn showed the afternoon temperature at twenty-eight degrees Fahrenheit. Maggie immediately knew that translated to negative 2.2 Celsius.

She observed the chicken coop surrounded by a hole-laden wire fence. Ten birds were crammed inside the small coop trying to avoid the cold, dry air. Then she went to the barn. She knew they had a horse and a few pigs and cows, so she went in to check them out.

Once inside, she heard a voice from the back of the barn. "Is that you, Little Missy? Come on back here. We need to talk," yelled Fred.

Maggie walked through hay, dirt, and smell while dodging the manure that blocked her way.

"Hello Fred. I see you're comfortable," Maggie said.

Fred was sitting on a pile of hay with a bottle of whiskey in his hand. He poured some of the whiskey into a glass. "You bet I am," Fred took a big gulp. "I'm takin' the day off. You too, but tomorrow I put you to work."

"What do you want me to do?"

"You know how to shovel manure, milk cows, feed chickens, and such? If not, you gonna learn. You ain't livin' for free around here Little Missy. You got to earn your keep."

"I suppose I can do all that. So, what are you going to do?"

"Shut up, Little Missy. Never talk back to me like that. I'll put you in your place like I do that other woman. Now, get out."

Maggie slowly turned around and walked out of the barn. She wasn't frightened of Fred. She knew she could handle him one way or another.

Maggie did not eat much of the pork feast. After dinner, Sally brought her a couple of new books to read. She went to her room after dinner and started to quickly scan through *How to Farm. A Profitable Life*. She was almost finished with the book when she heard an argument brewing. She put her ear against the door and tried to listen.

Fred was wearing a white sleeveless t-shirt. He reeked of whiskey and body odor. "Why you spend my money like that woman?" He grabbed Sally by the shoulders, then he used his right hand to slap her hard across her left cheek. "Now, I got no money for whiskey, and I'm out! You're a stupid woman."

"Stop Fred! You're drunker than a skunk. Margaret needs books. I bought her a couple of books. She's really smart, not a dumb shit like you. Get out of my house!" Sally got out of his grip and ran to the other side of the room.

Fred tackled her to the floor from behind. He turned her around and threw a hard-fisted punch, striking her in the right eye, causing her eye to swell up blue and her nose to bleed.

"Little Missy's the dumb shit. Tomorrow she starts the rest of her life shovelin' manure."

He put his hands around her neck and started to squeeze her throat shut.

While Sally was struggling to breathe, she heard a loud high voice.

"Leave her alone, Fred. It wasn't hard to figure out that you are the biggest dumb shit I have ever met." Maggie said as she stood confidently by her bedroom door.

"What you say, Little Missy? I think this one's had enough. I told you never to talk back like that, so now it's your turn," Fred said, as he got off Sally.

Maggie closed the door of her room and locked it. She got up on her bed and reached underneath her mattress. Now she waited for Fred to break down the door.

After three violent crashes the door shattered open. Fred stood there with his bloodshot eyes gleaming. "This is a great night. Two women put in their place in one…What?"

Maggie held the revolver with two hands. She fired three times hitting Fred in the chest with every shot. He looked down at his bleeding chest and fell to the floor.

Sally ran into the room and reached down to feel Fred's neck. "Oh my God! You shot him! He's dead!" she was hysterical. "Where did you get the gun? What am I supposed to do?"

Maggie got out of bed. "Calm down Sally. I told you I shot my Mom. It would make sense that I had a gun."

Sally was still screaming, "No, you were imagining that. What should I do? What should I do? Come on, think Sally."

"Maybe we should bury him. That's what they usually do when a guy dies."

"That's right. You're smart, Margaret. Let's bury him out in the fields. Nobody ever comes around here. They won't find him for months, or years, or ever. Good idea Margaret, I have a sleeping bag. We can put him in that and bury him. Get your big coat because it is freezing out there."

The two girls rolled Fred's remains into the sleeping bag. Sally used some old towels to wipe up the blood on the floor then threw them in the bag with the body. She zipped the sleeping bag up, and they dragged the wrapped-up corpse out the front door. They dragged the remains to an old wooden carriage near the barn.

"Help me get it into the back."

"I'll try. You know I'm only seven."

"You're seven going on thirty-seven."

Sally went into the barn and in a few minutes, she came back out with the horse, a flashlight, and a lantern. She handed the lights to Maggie and hooked up the horse to the cart. She went back in and soon returned with two shovels. They climbed into the back of the cart and then they both moved up into the front of the carriage as Sally took the reins.

"We should go out there about a half mile. Nobody will find him," Sally said.

"That ground is going to be cold and hard. I read that you should dig the grave six feet deep."

"Do you think this bastard deserves six feet?"

"The book said, if you don't, wild animals might dig up the dead person," Maggie answered.

"I'm not sure there's an animal alive that could stomach this asshole."

The Colorado night was clear. Millions of bright stars helped the lantern and flashlight brighten the scene. A cold blistering wind was blowing across the plains, turning their faces red. The snow gloves they wore lost their protection quickly as the temperature was a frigid nineteen degrees Fahrenheit.

They cleared away a ten-foot circle of snow. Sally's right eye was still half closed and there was a dark purple welt underneath. She had a piece of tissue in her right nostril to try to stop the bleeding. She started to dig into the cold hard earth, and she eventually got the hole to an oval one-foot deep.

Maggie asked, "Why did you marry this guy, Sally?"

"You know, I was young and stupid. Now, I'm older and still stupid."

"At least you were smart enough to get a divorce, or was it me that got you a divorce?"

"Funny, girl." Sally was getting winded. "I'm getting tired. Do you think you could dig for a bit?"

"I can try, and you know I'm only seven."

"I know, I know. We only got five feet to go."

Maggie got in the hole and tried to dig. "I think when we're done here, we should leave right away. Do you think his family will come to look for him?"

"He doesn't have much of a family. In fact, they hate him more than I do," Sally said as she took the shovel back from Maggie.

"I hate that Hatfield name. We need to change that at once," Maggie said.

"Me too. It's just a name. Do you have any ideas?"

Maggie said, "I never understood this maiden name thing. The woman bears the child, raises the child, and does all the work. The child should be named after the mother not the father."

Another cold breeze iced at their skin. The windchill made the air feel like a mere nine degrees.

"I agree with that for sure. Thank God we never had kids. Putting another monster like that into the world would be bad."

"Why didn't you have kids?"

"We tried a couple of times. I guess his sperm was too drunk to work right. Oops, I'm not supposed to talk like that around a child."

"I know all about sex, Sally."

Sally kept digging, "Look, we got almost three feet now,"

"So, what is your maiden name?"

"My grandparents came to the United States from France long ago. They had an odd name, even in France. It was Evolution. They shortened it when they came here to try to make it sound more American."

"*L'évolution, c'est le changement.*"

"What did you say, Margaret?"

"*L'évolution, c'est le changement.* I said, evolution means change in French."

Sally stopped digging. "Don't tell me you speak French."

"*Je fais. Ma mère m'a donné des dossiers. Les disques m'ont appris.*"

"In English," Sally said.

"If you're French, shouldn't you speak it? I said in French, my Mom got me some French records. The records taught me. I also speak backwards."

"Okay, What's that?"

"I can speak sentences backwards. Sometimes you can find hidden meanings in words, like your maiden name."

"What would Evolution be backward?"

"You said they shortened it. Did they shorten it to Evol?"

"Yes."

Maggie smiled. "Now, I could easily live my life with that name."

"Let me see, Evol backwards," Sally thought. "L, O, V, …love. My name is Sally Love."

Maggie thought for a second, then said, "Mom, I think the hole is deep enough. Let's throw him in. We're going to get frostbite if we stay out here much longer."

The two girls did that, then they filled the grave with icy dirt. They quickly got back into the carriage, then rode back to the house.

"You called me Mom. That wasn't my first vision of motherhood, burying my dead husband with my daughter," Sally said with a shiver.

"We need to leave this place. Do you have a plan?" Maggie asked.

"I have a cousin in California. Let's sleep for a while, then we can leave in the morning. I have some secret money left to get us out of here. I'll call my sister. She has a farm near Fort Morgan, and I can sell her the animals for cheap. That should get us through until I get a job."

"I guess you're starting all over, Mom."

"No, we are starting all over. We are going to be Sally and Margaret. No wait, I mean we are starting over as Sally and Maggie Love."

Ole' Bill the truck was puttering up Interstate 70 in the far-right lane. Even the slowest big rigs were quickly passing them on the left.

"Are we going too slow?" Maggie asked.

Sally replied, "This is as fast as this thing will go. I hope we can make it to Vail.

"I read about this in some of my books. Are we taking a road trip?"

"I think so. This is my first one. Never been up in these mountains before."

"It's so beautiful up here. I know I haven't seen much, but Mom, is all the world this wonderful?"

"Well, I haven't seen that much of the world either. I can tell you that this is the most beautiful place I have ever seen."

A light snow started to fall. Tiny snowflakes hit the windshield of the truck, making the whole scene seem even more magical. To their left, evergreen pine trees were reaching high into the sky, firmly imbedded into the white snow-covered hills. On the right, the same trees were coming out of a brown soil with just patches of snow about. The now missing sun was trying to ruin the view by melting the snow on the south side. As the freeway veered to the left, a large snowcapped mountain appeared behind all the trees and hills. They approached a green sign on the right that read, *Vail Pass SUMMIT, EVEL 10,662 FT.*

"I hope we can make it to Vail. I don't know what a summit is, but we should be close. This piece of junk is starting to heat up, and I think I see smoke coming out of the tailpipe," a nervous Sally said.

"A summit is the highest point of a mountain. I think it is going to be downhill all the way until we get to Vail."

"Good, we'll stop there. We need to get some water and antifreeze into this crappy truck. Then we will get something to eat and find a place to sleep. We didn't get much rest last night."

"Can we get Chinese, please," Maggie begged.

"Okay, if we can find a place, Chinese it is."

︎

They found a motel near the freeway. The small room they rented had two full-sized beds with a wooden floor and wood paneling on the walls. The ceiling was covered with an off-white stucco popcorn. The TV was blaring an episode of The Andy Griffin Show.

"I'm turning this thing off. We need to get some rest so we can get an early start in the morning," Sally ordered.

"Mom, I know we're going to Southern California, but that's a big place. Where in Southern California?"

"My cousin lives in a place called Reseda. I think it is near Los Angeles, or part of Los Angeles, something like that. I don't know for sure."

"That's in the San Fernando Valley. Are the people nice there?"

"I suppose. I've never been there. It's time for sleep, Maggie. Good night."

Sally turned off the light and fell right to sleep.

︎

Maggie didn't sleep. She had a feeling she had been in this hotel before. Then she thought she saw a man emerge in the darkness.

"Hello Maggie. You've had an appalling last few days," the man said.

"Mom, get up. Mom, there's a man in our room."

The Angel turned on the bathroom light. "Your new mom is going to sleep for a while, Maggie. Don't bother to wake her."

"Get out of here mister. I have a gun." Maggie looked at the man, "Wait a minute. What's with the trench coat and hat?"

"It's cold outside. The gun won't do you much good now." The Inspector slowly walked near the bed. He pulled a pack of cigarettes out of his coat and sat at the foot of her bed. He lit the cigarette. "I like the menthol kind of these the best. I'd offer you one, but I think you're too young."

"I am young alright but not too young to shoot you." Maggie reached under her mattress and pulled out the revolver.

"That won't do you any good without these." The Inspector reached into his coat again then showed her two bullets.

"Mom, get up. There's an inspector guy in here. I think he's some kind of an angel."

He looked at the little girl with a surprised look on his face. "Wait, how did you know who I am? That's not right. Your memory was supposed to have been wiped clean of me."

Maggie put down the gun. "Nobody wipes my memory clean. Lawrence, yes, I know you. You are Inspector Lawrence, the Angel."

"Every time I meet you Maggie, you amaze me more. That is not supposed to happen."

"It is happening, inspector guy." Maggie was no longer afraid.

"I do have to ask you a few questions. Do you know what repenting means?"

"Sure, it is when a person expresses sincere regret or remorse for something they have done."

"I thought you'd know that. Do you repent for killing your first Mom or Fred Hatfield?"

"No way. My Mom trained me and made me kill her. That Fred guy was beating my other Mom. I killed him because I knew I was next."

"Right about both. But since you feel no remorse, I have no choice. I'm not going to make you suffer this time."

"Why would you want to make me suffer?"

"Believe me, Maggie, that's the last thing I want to do. I just pray someday you will repent. Let's do this quickly. Do you repent for killing them?"

"No."

"Are you sure you have no remorse?"

"Yes."

The Inspector reached over and gently put his hand on Maggie's forehead. Maggie's mind exploded.

IV. THE ANGEL

WHAT THE CONSUL IS AND WHAT THEY ACTUALLY DO IS VERY HARD to describe to a person from the Below World. Yes, I have told you the Consul comprises three Female Beings and two Male Beings, but first, I need to tell you about all the other Beings that spend their eternity in the Bliss. Of course, we have no bodies. We cannot see with eyes because we have no eyes. We cannot hear with ears, speak with tongues, or feel the touch with fingers. How could we? We have no bodies of mere flesh and blood. All we possess is the inner soul. With our souls we can see closer than the most powerful microscope and further than the biggest telescopes floating in space. Our souls can hear any sound whenever we need. If a Being in the Bliss wants music, any song, work, or piece can be enjoyed at any time through the powerful feelings of the soul.

If a body from the Below World could see us, I think they would see a bright light in the middle of a circle, one meter in diameter. The light would dim as it neared the circumference of the sphere with a brilliant thin hose of sparking light circling the outer edge.

The members of the Consul's vivid light shines a little bit brighter because they have to spend their eternity orbiting high above the heavens in vibrant view of the entire Bliss population. The Consul members are constantly working. They are making, examining, and computing thousands of decisions in what the Below World calls a minute. They have a big decision to make right now. Should they terminate Maggie Love's soul or give me another chance to save her?

It wasn't unusual for an Inspector to get a fourth chance to save a soul and I easily got that, but I needed to get results fast because a fifth chance would be much more difficult to obtain. I learned a lot about Maggie while examining her childhood. Some people are dealt a bad deck in life, and soon crumble into worlds of almost lifeless despair. In my entire career as an inspector, I have never seen anyone that was dealt a worst deck than Maggie. The last examination proved that. Now, I needed to go later into her life.

I needed to find out if an elder Maggie was still Maggie Love.

4. In Her Eighties

MAGGIE WOKE UP.

The spinning room didn't bother too her much. There were two black metal rails on each side of her small bed, and she hung on tightly to each rail as the spinning increased, then slowed, then increased even more. When the zigzagging ride reached its peak, Maggie could not see through the dizzying blur that surrounded her. She could easily pick up the strong smell of urine, medications, and stale body order. As the spin started to slow, Maggie could hear two men talking above her bed. They were speaking in French.

"*This is that new one with all the history,*" said the man. He was obviously a native French speaker.

The other replied, also in French, "*She just got here. Is this the one that beat that murder rap? I didn't think her name was Susan Grey.*"

"*She is the one. She was on trial for the murder of my great uncle. This old hag couldn't kill anyone. There was a mistake made and they quickly found the real murderer. I'm going to make this one pay a big price.*" The man looked at the chart that hung near the foot of the bed. "*It says here that she is eighty-three years old. She is one of the unlucky ones. Her Alzheimer's did not respond to the medication.*"

Maggie could hear the men talking. She did not yet understand what it was all about. The memories were coming back into her head too slowly. She did know she was in France, and the place seemed awfully familiar. She also sensed it was only her in the room with the two men.

The taller heavyset man in his thirties was dressed in white scrubs, and his hair was cut into a military style crew cut. He said to the other younger man, "*She doesn't look eighty-three. All that brown color in her hair and those big green eyes make her look more like she is about sixty years old.*"

"You're right about that, Sir. How did she end up here?" Hugo was an orderly intern and was much shorter and younger than Clement. The kid was quite a contrast to the older manager. He wore the same white scrubs.

"*This is just what I heard. Maybe just rumors, but most probably true. When she beat the murder charge an upset prosecutor felt she, well, got away with murder. He had her committed and locked up in a nursing home outside of Paris. She escaped in just two days. That was twenty years ago and believe it or not, they just caught up with her and brought her here now*"

"*Will she escape from here, Clement?*" Hugo asked.

"*No way, not with our special brand of discipline.*"

The first memory came back. Maggie now knew where she was. It was a facility just south of the city of Orleans, a French city about one-hundred and thirty kilometers south of Paris. The institution that now surrounded her was built to hold elderly patients that were problematic, crazy, and susceptible to escape. Some of the residents were actual prisoners that were too old and sick to be held in the French penal system. It was more practical to hold these patients in this modern Alcatraz for old folks.

Suddenly while lying in her bed more memories came back. She knew exactly what to say, "Is that you, Brucie? Did my little Brucie finally come to see his old Nana?"

"*You speak English Hugo. What did she say?*" asked Clement.

"*I think she said, she's your Nana. She called you Brucie.*"

"*I'm not Brucie. Who's Brucie?*"

"*She thinks you're Brucie. I don't know who Brucie is either. She's got Alzheimer's. You'd think they would have a cure for that by now. It's 2039 for pete's sake,*" Hugo said.

"*They do have a cure, and you know it only works on twenty-six percent of patients. It doesn't work on the dumb ones.*"

Maggie said with a twinkle in her eyes, "Oh Brucie. Your Nana isn't so dumb. Please bring me a nice cup of hot cocoa with extra sugar, please Brucie?"

"*Hugo, what did she say?*"

"*She said she wants some hot cocoa with extra sugar.*"

Clement knelt close to Maggie's face and whispered, "*We have some big shots from the government here for a few days. That means you get a few days of slack. After that, you play by my rules. I run this place Susan Grey or whatever your name is. No cocoa for you."*

Maggie said in French, *"Whatever you say, Brucie. I like mine with a little extra sugar."*

Clement got up and spoke softly to Hugo, *"Keep your eye on this one."*

"What's she going to do? She's got Alzheimer's, and she is in stage four, so it says on the chart."

"Alzheimer's my ass, and just in case, find out who this Brucie is."

Maggie knew what she had to do. The plan was already written in her head. Maggie was almost positive she had been through all of this before.

She spent her first day in the nursing home learning the landscape of the place, and she also kept the Alzheimer's act going with perfection. She made everyone believe that she was always confused and out of touch with reality. She needed a few more days of playing this role before her first visitor would arrive.

The *Chateau Secure* was built in an industrial area in the city of Orleans in 2031 to secure its very disruptive clientele. At capacity, the nursing home held fifty-two patients, and everyone had a private room with a hospital bed, a dresser, and a small toilet. There were two very small security cameras on opposite sides of each room near the ceiling.

In the center of the complex was a large living area with a few lounge chairs, a bookcase filled with tattered old books, and some old worn-out board games stacked up on top of the case. They had a dining area with five large tables and chairs for the patients that were able to remember the dining times. Maggie now knew the layout of the place. It was easy for her because she felt she had been here before, and the déjà vu in her memory was still fresh. The important thing that the staff at this facility did not know was that Maggie had planned to be caught and brought to this home. Now that she was here, Maggie had some important and also, for her, some very fun work to do.

The staff was run by professional orderly/nurse named Clement Dubois, and the ship he ran made a Mexican prison look like a Caribbean resort.

Torture and starvation were commonly used to keep the residents in order. When corporal punishment was dished out, it was done in a special soundproof room with no cameras. Clement was the torture master, but he had also trained a few members of his staff the hideous practices as well. He taught them how to inflict pain, leaving little-to-no bruising on their elderly bodies. Maggie knew what was going on, and that was the only reason that she was here. She wanted to experience this treatment for herself. She accomplished this by spending a few hours following Clement around the nursing home, calling him Brucie, over and over again.

Clement had Hugo bring Maggie into the little special room he called The Boardroom. It was small and dimly lit with only a chair and a weird-looking machine with long wires on a small end table near the chair.

Clement closed and locked the door. *"Put this blindfold around her eyes, then you watch and learn. I will need you to do this soon."*

Hugo put the black blindfold on Maggie, tied it securely around the back of her head, then sat her down on the chair.

"Should we be doing this to an old lady? She's got Alzheimer's. Will she even remember this?" Hugo asked.

"Shut up Hugo, and do as you're told," Clement scolded. *"The only thing these so-called patients understand is pain. Now listen, when you slap them, do it with an open hand and hit them right below the cheek bone."*

Clement used his right hand to slap Maggie hard across the face. *"Did you see that, Hugo? Maximum pain and no bruise, just a little redness. Now you try."*

Hugo said in French, *"I don't know sir, she's just an old lady. Why can't you get someone else to train at this?"*

"You know we have a twenty-nine percent unemployment rate here in France. If you want this cushy job, better do as you're told!"

Hugo stood in front of Maggie and gently slapped her.

"Harder you moron!" Clement yelled. *"Do it or get out, I have four hundred plus people that want your job."*

Hugo closed his eyes and slapped Maggie much harder.

"That's much better. She felt that one." Clement grabbed the wires coming out of the strange machine that looked like an ancient radio. *"Now this is the next step. They used to use this on crazies in the old times. It is a brain*

shocker called an ECT contraption. They thought it helped people with crazy problems by frying their brains to hell. It was outlawed a few years ago, but I know it works because I use it to keep these old fogies in order. The best thing about this gadget is that it leaves no marks or bruises."

Clement used a damp towel to moisten Maggie's wrists, wrapped some wires around them, then took the remaining wires and attached them to Maggie's head. *"Give them orders before you shock them. Loud in their ears."* He got close to Maggie's left ear and screamed, *"Never call me Brucie again!"* he repeated, *"Never call me Brucie again."*

He reached over and turned on the machine. A few lights came on, along with a soft humming sound.

"Now, turn this knob to the right up to two hundred for four seconds. The water on her wrists makes it work better."

The machine threw two-hundred volts of electricity through Maggie's brain and body.

"Did you see her get all shaky," Clement said excitingly. *"She is still shaking like a British Nanny. That was perfect. She's going to obey me for a while. Remember, use this machine on the women only. Men just get the slap."*

Hugo asked, *"Why is that, sir?"*

"Do I have to tell you everything? Women are a big pain in the ass, and it is so unfair that they live longer than us men. I'm going to change that."

"What do you want me to do now?"

"Get her back to her bed. She's going to sleep for a time."

"Why is she smiling?"

Maggie said softly, *"Is that you Brucie? Why is this blindfold over my eyes? Your Nana wants to see her little Brucie."*

Clement said angrily, *"She's delirious. Get her out. And find out who this Brucie is."*

⁓⁓⁓

When Visitor's Day arrived, Maggie got out of bed early and looked out the door. She was not surprised to see the young blond nurse Hugo coming towards her room with an older, familiar lady. Maggie got back into her bed.

They both entered Maggie's room and Hugo said in English, "Okay Susan, you have a visitor. She says she's your sister."

Maggie replied, "Where is Brucie? You're not my Brucie."

"No, this is not Brucie. This is your sister Laura." Hugo turned to Laura, "Her Alzheimer's is very bad. You can sit with her for a while, but all she talks about is this Brucie character. Do you know who that is?"

Laura sounded like she was acting. "I have no knowledge of any Bruce. Although I haven't seen her in some time, maybe Brucie is like an imaginary son, or something."

Hugo lowered the safety bars on the sides of Maggie's bed and said, "Talk to her all you want. Visiting time is one hour."

Hugo left and closed the door while Laura sat on the end of the bed, "Hello Big Sis. How in the hell do you stay so slim?"

Maggie replied, "Did you find my Brucie?" Then she placed her mouth close to Laura's ear and whispered, "Did you bring me what I asked for?"

Laura reached into her blouse and took out an eight-inch by eight-inch tablet.

"Put it behind you, to block those cameras," Maggie said.

Maggie began to move her hands rapidly above the computer using a special sign language. The strange movements of her hands and the unusual signs she made was not American or French sign language. The complex signs were letters and phrases that only Maggie and her computer could understand.

"Okay, Laura. I'm on the network now."

Maggie wasn't directly on the nursing home or local network. Instead she was on a special network that was broadcast worldwide. Only a few members knew of it and sometimes referred to it as HWN (Hackers Worldwide Network).

"Act like you're talking to me. Just a few more seconds," Maggie whispered.

"Okay," Laura said, "Why didn't you come home when Mom died?"

Maggie continued to wave her hands and fingers wildly above the tablet. "I've hacked into the nursing home network now. I found my room, and now I am turning cameras and audio off."

Maggie gave Laura a big hug. "How have you been little Sis. We can talk now. You know I couldn't come back eleven years, six months, and five days ago when Mom died. I was on trial here in France."

Maggie's sister did not look like her at all; she had light olive skin and short black hair, much like an Hispanic woman. At sixty-five, she didn't look much younger than her eighty-three-year-old sister. She handed Maggie a death announcement card. There was a picture of a young blond woman, and the card said, "A Caring Mother, Sally Love, 1941 to 2027."

"Destroy this," Maggie said. "I can't be associated with that name."

"I will. I just thought you might want to see it. Now you promised me this. You said you would come back to the states with me if I helped you. I got your tablet in here. How did it get through a metal detector? You know they have guards out there and most of them have guns."

"The tablet got through because it isn't metal. Don't worry about the guards. I control this entire place now."

Laura smiled at her sister. "You look so good Maggie. Why do you need to control this place? You have enough money for the best lawyers, and they would get you out of here in five seconds."

"What fun is that? A girl has got to have fun sometimes; that's what keeps me young. Besides, I have some especially important work to do here. Let me show you something." Maggie started to wave her hands over the computer. "Listen to the intercom."

A woman's voice came on loudly over the nursing home's sound system in French. It said, *"Brucie, paging Brucie. Hugo the intern is paging Brucie."*

Laura laughed. "That is French, I think it said someone is looking for Brucie. There is no Brucie here, is there?"

Maggie said, "This is going to be so much fun."

~~~

Hugo was cleaning one of the rooms when Clement finally found him. *"Did you page me? I heard you paged me."*

"It wasn't me; I heard the intercom say I paged Brucie."

"I'm not Brucie. Something funny is going on around here. Anyway, I need to talk to you. You are doing a terrible job, so I'm demoting you to the night shift. Go home and come back at nineteen hundred on the dot."

A frustrated Hugo said, *"I thought I was doing great. What did I do wrong?"*

"I'll tell you tonight during your training."

Hugo couldn't understand why Clement waited till the end of his shift to tell him about his demotion. He had two hours until his new shift started. He decided he would just wait it out in the employee lunchroom. The French economy was now near collapse. Soup kitchens and shanty towns were popping up all over the country. Hugo desperately needed this job just to survive. He would reluctantly do whatever his boss asked.

Hugo was making his rounds around twenty hundred hours when Clement appeared in the hall, he whispered to Hugo, *"Come with me to room forty-nine. We have a job to do."*

An ever-alert Maggie saw the two men go into the room three doors down from hers. She immediately got out her computer and hacked into the institution's video surveillance system. Maggie was not surprised to see that the video and audio for room forty-nine was turned off. She turned it back on but only received the feed through her device. She could see and hear everything in the room perfectly. There was an old grey woman sleeping on her back with her mouth open. Clement and Hugo were standing above her.

She heard Clement say, *"I've got the cameras turned off in here. This is just training now but every two weeks or so I'm going to tell you to do this."* Clement took out two syringes. *"The red one is for you to inject it into her veins."*

"What is it?" Hugo asked.

"It's Digoxin, and don't ask so many questions. Find a vein on this ugly broad's arm and do as you're told."

Hugo took the syringe and tried to find a vein. *"Shouldn't we put some alcohol on it first?"*

"No, we don't need that for these women. Just do it."

Hugo stuck the needle into the woman and pressed the plunger down, forcing the Digoxin into her.

"Now it shouldn't take much time. You gave her an extra-large dose. Her heart rate will slow down while her blood pressure increases. You wait till she starts to die; that's when you call me. I will be around. I'll come in and give her this." He took a blue syringe and injected the woman with the serum. *"This is Digibind, this is the antidote for the Digoxin. It should make her all better."*

"Why are we doing this?"

"I've done this twelve times already. Each time I come out a hero for saving their lives. The eight that died do not matter so much. They were going to die anyway."

"If they die, isn't that murder?"

"Do you want this job, Hugo? Let me try to explain. It's a win-win scenario. If they live, I'm a hero. If they die, we get rid of one of these worthless old hags."

IV. THE ANGEL • 4. In Her Eighties

"Looks like she's coming out of it."

"What's going on? Why are you men in my room?" the groggy woman asked.

"Hello Mrs. Douglas. We are here just to make sure one of our favorite residents is all right," Clement said.

"Why does my arm hurt so bad?"

"It's a little drafty in here. Hugo, turn up the heat."

Maggie watched the win-win scenario scene with delight. It was going to be a win-win for her also. This was so much easier, and so much more fun than she ever imagined. Her tablet was recording everything.

Clement arrived at his office at ten in the morning. He was going through some paperwork when a young blond nurse came in, "Good morning, Mr. Dubois. A delivery guy just brought you this."

She placed a large white and green Starbucks cup on his desk. The cup had the name Brucie written on it in green ink.

"What's this? I didn't order anything."

"The guy said it's a hot cocoa with a little extra sugar for Brucie."

"I'm not Brucie."

"Oh, I thought that was a new nickname or something. Everyone is calling you Brucie."

"Tell them to stop," Clement said with anger.

"I almost forgot; upper management wanted us to wear new name tags. They want us to display a friendlier ambiance here at work. I printed them up for everyone, so here is yours."

The name tag was written in French 'HELLO, MY NAME IS BRUCIE DUBOIS. HOW CAN I HELP YOU?'

"There it is again. Did you put that on there?" Clement asked with more anger.

"Hey, don't blame me. I just printed what the computer had in it. You'd better wear it. Upper management is poking around."

Maggie sat with her two new friends at a table near the kitchen. Maggie and the two white- haired women were watching various news reports and resident bulletins that were flashing on one of five big screens that were hanging about in the living and dining room areas of the home.

Donna Douglas was the first to speak, *"My arm hurts so bad. Something happened last night. Mr. Dubois and that intern were in my room."*

Maggie said, *"Did my Brucie come to visit you?"*

A woman with thick coke-bottle glasses named Mary told Maggie, *"Susan, you shouldn't call him that. I don't think he likes it."*

As Clement Dubois walked by Maggie, she said loudly, *"Sure he likes it. My Brucie came all the way from California in the United States just to see his Nana. Look at his nametag."*

"By George, it says Brucie. Good afternoon Brucie," Mary greeted.

"Hope you are having a nice day, Brucie." Donna added.

Clements eyes started to glow red with anger. He yelled at the top of his lungs, *"Listen everyone! No one, either resident or staff, is allowed to call me Brucie. As punishment, no lunch will be served to all residents and if I hear that name again, no dinner also!"*

"Oh dear," Mary said. *"I'm so hungry."*

Maggie got up from the table. *"Don't worry. He is just kidding us. I know my Brucie would never do that."*

She headed quickly to her room. There was important computer work to be done.

An hour later three guards entered the dining room holding four big white bags with pictures of grapes and olives and the words *Jardin d'oliviers* printed on them.

A middle-aged burley guard dressed in a blue and green uniform yelled out, *"Come and get it everyone! Lunch is served! More on the way."*

Clement heard all the commotion and ran out of his office to the dining area. *"Hey Tomas, what are you doing? I didn't say you guards could come in here."*

Tomas the guard replied, *"Screw you, Brucie. The delivery guy promised us a huge tip if we hand-deliver. In this economy, every franc counts."*

"But they don't get lunch today."

"Looks like they do. The delivery guy said you paid for it."

As the bewildered residents slowly moved towards the dining area, Mary yelled out, *"It's the Olive Garden. I love the Olive Garden!"*

"It's my favorite," Donna said. "I would kill for their lasagna."

As the guards handed out the plastic containers of Italian delicacies, Maggie knew her order had arrived. The time was perfect, and she waved her hands over her computer to text her sister.

Susan: Are you here Little Sis?

Laura: Yes, and ready.

Susan: I'm turning off the metal detectors for twenty seconds.

Laura: See you in a bit.

Maggie met her sister at the door of her room and quickly closed it.

Laura handed her a large decorative gift bag. "Here is your order. I don't want to know why you need that thing, but what's with the knitted red sweater?"

Maggie said, "The less you know the better. One more thing while you're here."

Maggie put her tablet close to her right eye and snapped a picture. She showed it to Laura. "How does it look?"

"It looks green."

"I have to put this in this raisin farm's employee data base. I can change it just enough so they could never associate it with any of my aliases. How does the name Gracie sound?"

"I see nothing and hear nothing. So, we go home tonight?'

"Yes, you have the passports and boarding passes I got you? I have a little more work, then home to California."

"See you at the airport Big Sis."

Clement Dubois watched with resentment as the residents and staff feasted on the lunch. He knew he was losing control of the place, and it all started when this Susan Grey was admitted. Alzheimer's or not, something had to be done quickly. Something diabolical had to be done, tonight.

~~~

At twenty-three hundred that night, Clement found Hugo sleeping in the employee lunchroom. He was working his shift alone.

"*Hugo, wake up. You're supposed to be working not sleeping,*" Clement said, trying to keep his voice soft so as not to wake any of the sleeping elderly.

"*Oh, what? Sorry, I just dozed off during my break.*"

"Shut up. We got work to do. Go get that Susan Grey and take her to The Boardroom."

"That poor woman is going to get it again? Come on, she's got Alzheimer's"

"Alzheimer's my ass. Now do what you are told or go check into a shanty town."

Maggie was escorted by Hugo into The Boardroom. She was carrying the gift bag.

Hugo said to Clement, "She insisted on bringing that bag. She says she has a gift for you."

"Lock the door and get her in the chair. She is getting the gift. I'm giving her triple treatment. First slaps, then brain fry, then we take her to her room and inject her with Digoxin. I may be a little late with that antidote."

Maggie did not sit down. She looked at Clement and said, "Is Brucie mad at his old Nana? I knitted you this nice red sweater."

She took the sweater out of the bag to show him.

"Sit her down, Hugo," Clement said with rage.

Maggie quickly pulled her 38 Special Smith and Wesson revolver from under the sweater and stuck it in Clements's temple. She fired once. The bullet went in one side of his head, tearing his brain to pieces as it journeyed out the other side. Blood squirted out from both sides of his head as he made a sloppy gurgling sound and fell to the floor.

"Good night, Brucie," Maggie said.

Then she looked at the stunned Hugo and pointed the gun at him.

"You know, you're a cute young guy, but you shouldn't be injecting the elderly with dangerous drugs."

Hugo stuttered and shook as he talked, "No-no, he made me do it."

"Yes, but I have to stop you from hurting more people."

"You're going to-to-to kill me?"

Maggie didn't answer because she didn't need to. She fired twice, hitting Hugo both times in the forehead. As he fell to the floor Maggie continued to talk to him in English.

"Okay Hugo, I did kind of like you, but you know what you are."

She reached into the bag and took out a white nurses' uniform. Taking off her clothes she said, "You two made this so easy for me. This room is so soundproof, nobody heard the shots, and there are no cameras. I've had this gun for a long time, and I am pretty positive this is the last Dubois I need to kill with it."

She wiped the gun with dead Clements's hand, then placed it in the position it would have landed if he dropped it.

Maggie got into the uniform and put on a nametag. It said in French, *HELLO, MY NAME IS GRACIE ALLEN. HOW CAN I HELP YOU?*

"And Hugo, at zero-nine hundred this morning, everyone here at the old folks barn and everyone at the Orleans Police Station are going to get to see a video of you and Clement almost killing that poor woman."

Finally, Maggie put a white nurse's cap on her head.

"You know I love a murder-suicide scenario so Hugo, I kind of made up some e-mails and it seems like you rejected Clement's gay advances. He loved you so much, and he could not take the rejection, so he shot you twice in the head, then he turned the gun on himself."

Maggie unlocked the door and left, making sure the door was securely locked again behind her, then calmly walked out of the main entrance of the ward. When she got to the guard station, she looked into a camera with her right eye, then she said to a woman guard behind a monitor, *"Hello I'm Gracie. I'm new here."*

The guard looked at the iris on her computer screen, *"Yes, you are Gracie Allen. Today was your first day."*

Maggie said with as much cheer as she could, *"Yes, it was a wonderful day. I enjoyed it so much. I hope to see you tomorrow."*

"Good night, ma'am. She turned to another female guard and said to her, "You know, when I get older, I want to look like that."

"Don't we all," the other guard said. *"Don't we all."*

◦⎯⎯◦

Laura and Maggie were sitting comfortably in their large first-class seats. Maggie had the window seat. They were traveling at 90,000 feet above sea level during the eleven-plus hour flight from Paris to Los Angeles, California. Laura had dozed off while Maggie was open-eyed and alert. She looked at her sleeping sister and felt this was not right.

She shook Laura gently. "Laura, get up. I need to tell you something."

"What is it, Maggie?" Laura was half asleep.

"I really appreciate you helping me. You are the best sister I could ever want. Thank you so much."

"Sure Maggie. I got a free first-class trip to Paris, and I got to see my always-changing big sister."

"I just want you to know, I love you very much Laura Love-Hernandez."

"Maggie, are you crying? I never thought I'd see the day when Maggie Love cried. I have to use the restroom."

"Goodbye, Laura."

"What are you talking about? I'll be back in a minute."

Maggie whispered to herself, "No you won't."

A short grey-haired man opened the overhead bin above Laura's seat. He placed his trench coat and fedora hat inside and closed it. Then he sat down in Laura's seat.

"Excuse me," Maggie said. "My sister is sitting there."

The Inspector replied, "Hello Maggie."

"Oh, it's you Inspector. Here to kill me again? It is just my luck, everybody gets a Guardian Angel, but mine wants to kill me."

"I told you those kinds of angels don't exist. It is amazing; every time I tell them to wipe your memory extra clean, you seem to remember more."

Maggie got mad. "I told you, you, they can't wipe my memory clean. I will not let them. I'm confused at first when this all starts, but eventually I figure it out."

"Okay but anyway, I have a job to do. You just killed two men. Do you regret that in any way?"

"No way, that monster killed eight people that we know of, maybe dozens more."

"True, but what about the young boy Hugo. Did he deserve to die?"

"You know what he was."

"Collateral damage?" the Inspector asked.

"Yes, collateral damage. Are you going to shoot me this time?"

The Inspector asked, "Are you sorry and do you repent for these murders?"

"Fuck yourself." Maggie got angrier.

"You know it's not lady-like for an elderly woman to swear like that. Do you repent?"

"Cram it up your ass. Why don't you just throw me off the plane?"

IV. THE ANGEL • 4. In Her Eighties

"Not a bad idea."

The Inspector reached across Maggie and threw his fist through the small window, shattering it open. Then he released Maggie's seat belt. The pressure breach at 90,000 feet above sea level sucked Maggie's slim body outward, ripping off her left arm and shoulder as she passed through the window into the frigid atmosphere. At fifty-six below zero Fahrenheit, with the unlivable pressure and lack of oxygen, this would kill a human instantly. Maggie didn't die. She had to feel her blood surge out of control at the high pressure of 90,000 feet high. She had to feel the freezing temperature cut into her body and increase the pain of her missing arm and shoulder. Soon she reached terminal velocity, falling 157 feet per second. When her almost ten-minute trip would conclude, hitting the Atlantic Ocean, it would be like hitting rock hard concrete. The force would break her body into millions of smaller pieces.

Right before she contacted the water, Maggie's mind exploded.

V. THE ANGEL

I thought one of my missions as an Inspector was to administer a punishment if the examinee did not repent and feel sorrow for their victims and for the crimes they committed. The Consul felt my last punishment was way too insensitive for an Angel. I will have to be a little more lenient when giving Maggie her next penance. Getting forced off an airplane in flight at 90,000 feet above sea level might be a little severe, and they reprimanded me by giving me a major demerit. This is the first demerit I have ever received. I heard about Maggie's lone trial that happened at some unknown time in her life, but if I get one more demerit, I will have to go to trial also. If this happens, I could lose my Inspectorship and at worse, be forced to the Below World to live again as a new soul. My trial would have one advantage over Maggie's trial. We do not have lawyers here in the Bliss.

I easily got permission to give Maggie a fifth examination. I know I am closer, and this next exam should answer some key questions. This will be a crucial time in her life.

It was very unusual to get a fifth exam so effortlessly. So, I have a speculation. The Consul only wants to hear about repentance and rehabilitation during an examination. They do not listen much to all the trite details. So how did they learn about Maggie's recent punishment? When I was scolded, they seemed to know everything about every exam Maggie has had so far. I know some of the Beings in the Bliss will tune into examinations as a form of entertainment now and then, so this is my theory. The members of the Consul are fans of Maggie Love.

5. In Her Thirties

MAGGIE WOKE UP.

The spinning and dizziness were again extremely intense. The violent whirling turned Maggie's stomach. She could sense through all the dizziness that it was night because various electric lights were around, but what she really saw was 90 percent darkness. She was sitting up straight holding something circular with both hands. Maggie felt she was in motion, and as the spinning increased, she sensed a nauseating pain in her stomach. She coughed and threw up on her chest.

As the revolving decreased, she felt the forward motion increase. She was going much faster. Through the blur she saw something coming straight at her. Her instincts told her to hit a pedal on the floor with her right foot, so she pushed the pedal down hard. That was followed by a loud screeching sound from underneath her, then an impact that threw her forward into the circular object. When the forward motion had stopped, Maggie felt pain near her eyes where she hit the object. The circular object was a steering wheel.

Things started to clear up, but she still had no memories. There was a mirror above her to her right. She adjusted it so she could see her face. The reflection showed a young woman with dark-brown hair styled in a wraparound bun. One of the lenses of her brown thick-rimmed glasses had a crack from the impact. Her eyes were brown, but she felt there were foreign objects inside them.

Soon a stocky young Middle Eastern man appeared to her left. His accent was heavy. "Lady! What you do? You ran right in the back of my cab."

With still little memory, Maggie said, "I don't know what happened. I hit my head on the wheel."

Maggie noticed a flashing red light coming from behind. She tried to straighten up her hair.

The cab driver started to yell at a person from behind, "Policeman, you see what this crazy lady does. She smash up my cab. Put her under arrest. She a menace to society."

A tall, handsome police officer appeared in Maggie's window. "You alright, Ma'am? There's a little blood over your right eye."

"Yes, I'm fine," Maggie's memories were returning, and she realized the voice she used was wrong. She repeated with a nasally voice. "Yes, yes, very fine I am. Just a little shook up. I am very fine, yes I am, yes."

Maggie noticed the patch on the officer's left arm. It read, "*Metropolitan Police District of Columbia.*"

"Can you get out of the car, Ma'am? I need to see your license and registration."

Maggie noticed a yellow handbag on the passenger's seat. She opened it and searched for a license. She found it and more memories started to pound back into her head. She knew she was in Washington DC. She could not remember the time or date, but she sensed she had an appointment tomorrow morning. Maggie opened the door and tried to get out. As she stood, one final surge of dizziness shook the world around her, buckling her knees. The officer held her up before she fell.

"Have you been drinking ma'am? There's a little vomit on your suit."

"No, no. No drinking and driving. That is very bad," Maggie made her voice even more nasally. "Just shook up a little you know."

The cab driver practically spit, he was so mad. "That is very drunk lady. Look at my cab. Her car, little scratch. My cab all smashed up bad."

The red Volkswagen bug she was driving had a slightly crooked and dented front bumper. The rear end of the Yellow Cab was smashed, forcing the trunk to open.

Maggie handed the officer her license and registration, then she found a headkerchief in her bag and tried to wipe the puke off her green business suit.

"So, you're Molly Jones. Do you have an insurance card Miss Jones?"

"That is Ms. Jones. Yes, yes, insurance. Officer, I am a little confused from the crash. The impact, you know."

"Do you want me to call an ambulance?"

"No, no," Maggie then asked. "What time is it?

The officer looked at his watch. "It's 8:45."

V. THE ANGEL • 5. In Her Thirties

"And the date?"

"It is June 27th."

"I am sorry to be such a bother Mr. Officer but the year?"

"I'm sorry Miss, I mean Ms. Jones. You don't smell like alcohol, but I'm going to give you a brief sobriety test. Do you agree?"

"Yes, yes, test is fine, very fine."

The officer instructed Maggie to walk heel-to-toe for nine steps in a straight line while counting the steps out loud, then to turn around and repeat the nine steps. Maggie accomplished the procedure without the slightest waver.

"Okay Ms. Jones, wait here a minute."

The officer went over to the cab driver and talked to him for a while. Then he went to his car. Soon, he returned to Maggie.

"Here's the deal Ms. Jones, I'm citing you for following too close. Exchange information with Mr. Fazil and you can be on your way. Remember, drive safely."

Maggie said, "Yes, yes, Officer. I will drive very safely. A lot to do tomorrow, you know, working in our nation's capital. We must run the whole country from here. And Officer, oh I know I am such a bother, but what is the year?"

"Now, come on, it's 1988."

Maggie finished up with the complaining and whining Mr. Fazil. She got in her Volkswagen, started it up and drove off. She knew where she had to go. She had a rented three-bedroom house on Kennedy Street three miles away, and it had a basement.

<hr />

Everything was blurry. Maggie felt that she was very young, and she knew that she was walking up the stairs of the basement trying to be extra quiet with each step. She could hear her parents talking.

"Bob is not going to give up," Alison McLander said softly. "After what I did, they are never going to give up."

Her husband Rob answered, "We just have to keep moving. Eventually, Bob and his goons will give up."

"It's been six years. I dreaded the day we decided to work for that nonprofit."

"Yes, we should have known the whole thing was a scam. The Mestiño Society was just a way for Bob and his partners to make millions."

"I love horses, and I thought we were helping the wild mustangs of the west. I visited that little ranch they had in Illinois. They had four beautiful mustangs there. Why did you have to steal so much?" Allison asked for the hundredth time.

"I just wanted to hit them where it hurt, right in their wallets. The money is safe now. Maggie will have a good life."

"If she lives. What was that? Did you just hear something? I'm checking the basement."

Allison went to the basement stairs and turned on the light. She saw the five-year-old trying to hide about halfway up the stairs.

"Maggie!" Allison yelled. "You know you're not supposed to be up here. Get back to bed."

Maggie woke up from her dream in a slight sweat. She wasn't in a basement. She was in a bed in her house in Washington DC. She had the reoccurring dream again, and there wasn't a better time. She had a job interview with Congressmen Robert Baker early in the morning. The memory of that dream would be fresh in her mind.

The jobs Maggie took during her years in Washington were mostly clerical. With her photographic memory she could take dictation without writing down a thing. She always faked like she was writing shorthand, but to her, this was a waste of time, and with her typing speed of over two hundred words a minute, employment was easy for her to find around this town.

Some of these jobs gave Maggie access to the computers of the day, and she loved them. As the computers got better and faster, so did Maggie's hacking skills. When the internet came along, Maggie was in computer heaven. Her hacking was not to harm the internet or unprotected computers. She wanted to learn all she could, and she always needed information, not only for her entertainment, but she needed to find out who this Robert guy was. She also needed to know what the Mestiño Society was and Robert's connection to it. She spent hours a day, during and after work, searching for information to satisfy her always curious mind.

She hunted for the nonprofit for years with no results. Maggie knew her memories were accurate. It seemed this organization was wiped off the records like it never existed. With the more powerful computers, Maggie was able to hack into the National Archives of the United States. Still no luck on The Mestiño Society, so she took a different approach.

First, she searched horse ranches. Then, horse ranches in Illinois. She found a small one that was in operation between 1954 and 1961. They specialized in mustang preservation. The registered owner of the ranch was a man named Robert Fournier.

Her hacking was so good that she easily got into the FBI's criminal database. There, she found a Robert (Bob) Fournier. He had a couple of priors, one for armed robbery and another for felony domestic violence. It seemed he beat his wife quite regularly. He served two years in the federal prison in Marion, Illinois. After more digging at the federal library, she found a mugshot.

Maggie could remember faces as easily as she could remember facts. She knew the faces of all one hundred Senators and all four hundred and thirty-five Congressmen. When she saw the mugshot of a young Robert Fournier, she knew she had seen that face before. Speaking different languages often can be an advantage. She knew right away that Fournier translated from French to English was Baker.

Maggie always loved politics. When she made the decision to come to Washington eleven years ago, it was not just that. If most women do have women's intuition, Maggie had this gift times ten. Maggie knew there were answers in DC. Tomorrow she would find out for sure if Congressman Robert Baker was really Bob Fournier.

※

Maggie sat across from the slender Congressman sitting behind his big oak desk. He was balding and middle aged with a grey flop-over hairstyle to try to hide his bald spot. He had Molly's resume in his hands, reading it over.

"So, Molly Jones. The position, as you know, is to become my personal assistant. It requires long hours and low pay. We have a campaign starting soon and that means even more stress."

Maggie replied with a nasally voice, "Yes, yes. I am willing to endure everything, just for the chance to work for a United States Congressman."

"You're the last candidate I'm talking to. I have interviewed eight already. You have the experience. You do dictation, and you really type two hundred a minute?"

"Yes, on a slow day. Ha, Ha."

"What about computers?"

"Love them. Love Microsoft. I am very proficient in both Word and Excel."

"How tall are you, Molly?"

"Oh, Congressman. I am five foot eleven."

"That's two inches taller than me. Would you mind standing up for a minute and turn around."

Maggie did while saying, "Oh congressman, I am so embarrassed."

"Okay," Robert Baker said. "You get the job. Your voice is so annoying, but you've got a body that doesn't quit."

"Oh, thank you Congressman. I will work my hardest every day here in our nation's capital. I am so, so very happy."

"You can start on Monday, and one more thing, do you play the game?"

"The game?" Maggie asked.

"Yes, the game. I need someone who plays the game. Especially here in DC when I'm away from the wife."

"Yes, yes, the game. I'm exceptionally good at games."

"Very good, Molly. Get ready to work for the people of the great state of Illinois. I will see you first thing Monday morning."

As Maggie walked out of the office, she was positive she had found him. The facial features between this man and the mugshot were too exact to be a coincidence. Maggie had finally found the Bob that had plagued her dreams for years.

⁂

Maggie had been in character for over ten years. She played the part of Molly Jones most of the time, and if she did anything social, she tried to do that under the alias of Bonnie Dickerson. There was a man that lived three houses down from her. He had been asking her out for over two years and would not give up. Maggie finally gave in, and thought now might be a good time. She agreed to a walk in the park and a cup of coffee. This man did not know Bonnie Dickerson. She would have to go out with him as Molly Jones.

In June of 1988, Washington DC was having a record heat wave. Maggie wore a pair of blue denim jeans with a blue t-shirt and blue sneakers for the Saturday afternoon walk. She kept the nasally voice. "I did not say you could hold my hand. No, no, you are not my boyfriend you know."

James dropped her hand, "You know, if I was, we could share the same clothes. We are the exact same height."

James Cannon was a light-skinned African American who was the same height as Maggie. His black hair was short and trim. The thick-rimmed glasses on his face made him look a little nerdy. Because he was in such good physical shape, he was one of the few guys that could pull off the nerd look and the athletic look at the same time.

"Ha, ha, James, very funny," Maggie said sarcastically.

The heat made the walk-through Fort Totten Park a little uncomfortable. A cool wind blew past them as they walked through the scenery. The couple walked over a wooden bridge that led to a path surrounded by lush green trees. The branches spread over the path, the shade helping to protect them from the heat.

"Molly, it is so hot," James said. "Why don't we find an air-conditioned place and have lunch?"

"I said a walk and coffee only. No food, I did not say food."

"But I'm starving. You can spare an hour with me, no?"

Maggie knew she was making a mistake when she said, "If we have Chinese, I will go, but only Chinese."

"Do you know that 'Wok This Way' Restaurant?" James asked.

"Yes, yes, it is one of my favorites. Very authentic Mandurian cuisine."

"It's not too far. Let's wok that way."

The couple sat on wooden stools with a wooden table between them. Soon, a waitress brought them two servings of sesame chicken and brown rice. They both had a glass of white wine.

"We have so much in common, we should go out more often," James said.

Maggie asked, "What do we have in common?"

"Well, we both work for the government, we are both single, and we both love computers. Keep this quiet, but I've become a pretty good hacker. Have you ever tried hacking?"

"No, no, never tried. Very illegal activity," Maggie said with her most nasally voice.

"You know, Molly Jones, there is something different about you. I don't know why you keep up that nerdy appearance. You are really quite beautiful."

"No, no. Not beautiful. Just doing my best to help run this country here in our nation's capital."

"Who says stuff like that? Do you want another glass of wine?"

"I say these things because I am very, very dedicated. And no hacking. It is very illegal activity, James." Maggie knew she was making another mistake when she said, "Okay, one more glass."

After lunch, James paid the bill, got up and went behind Maggie. He pulled her chair back as she stood up and then said, "I've been thinking. I'll cut down on my hacking if you come over to my place and watch a movie with me."

"No, no. No movies. Hollywood puts out such trash nowadays."

"Come on, I got two videos," *Revenge of the Nerds II*" and "*Dirty Dancing*."

"No, nerds no. No nerds. Do not like the nerds. I have always wanted to see that *Dirty Dancing* movie."

"Great," he said as he walked her to the door.

When outside James said, "seven o'clock?"

Then he tried to give her a goodbye kiss.

Maggie blocked his face with her right hand. "No kissing. Not my boyfriend." Maggie knew she made her third mistake. "I will see you at seven."

※

Maggie got up before dawn on Sunday morning. She heard a slight snore from the man sleeping next to her. She quickly got up and got dressed.

"James, get up. I need to talk to you." Maggie's voice was still through the nose.

James sat up and groggily said, "What? Molly, good morning. You're up so early."

"I made some mistakes last night. I need you to forget this ever happened. I will be going away soon."

"What? Where are you going? You just got a new job."

Maggie got back into the Molly act, "You know, family issues to sort out. Yes, I have to go back."

"Where are you going? Maybe I can help, or I can wait for you."

"No, no. No helping. No waiting."

James said with frustration, "What are you talking about? I'm falling in love with you, and you are just going to leave?

"If you love me, then you must promise."

"Promise what?"

"That this night never happened. You know me only from small talk in the yard. People will question you."

"Last night was the greatest night of my life and you're just going to get up and leave?"

Maggie said sternly, "promise."

"I will, if you promise that I will see you again."

The déjà vu Maggie felt was overwhelming, "I promise."

"When?"

"I promise in the very near distant future."

"That's not good enough. I love you, Molly Jones."

Maggie stopped the nasal accent. "James, who am I? I may be Molly. Never ask why. Drop the why. Gee, join the Army, and add everything. E is for everything. I can never feel love. It is impossible for me to feel love, because I am love. Now, you need to learn Spanish."

"What is this, a riddle?"

Maggie left the house.

―――

Her new job started on Monday. She suspected with the long hours as Personal Assistant to the Congressman, there would be little time during the week. The *deja vu* in her mind also told her that after a long week of assisting Congressman Baker, her real job would start Friday night. Maggie wanted to get as much work done on this Sunday as possible.

Maggie needed the natural color of her hair back. She used baking soda and lemon juice to remove the dark brown dye. This would take a few days and a few more applications to get her hair back to the untreated color. In the meantime, she would wear her freshly styled, dark brown La Belle Époque wig to work.

While her hair dried, she changed into some pantyhose. Then a pair of short shorts with a flowered backless blouse. She stuffed her hair under a wig cap and put on her short blond curly wig. Then she dotted a few freckles on her face with a cosmetic pencil. The decision was red sneakers instead of red high heel shoes. She had some running around to do today.

Maggie looked at herself in a full-length mirror and said in her thick southern accent, "Woo wee girl! You one damn good-lookin' babe. This is gonna be a great day for Bonnie Dickerson."

She opened the garage door and backed her VW out to the street and drove the other way, away from James's house. She didn't worry about him too much. She knew he would keep his promise.

The shop was located about twenty miles south of her neighborhood. There were a few cars parked out front this early Sunday morning. Maggie had visited a few of these during her brief stint as an adult entertainer. She walked in and started to browse the merchandise.

Soon she was asked by a male employee, "Can I help you madam?" he noticed her short shorts. "Oh, I see. Do you have a special client tonight?"

Maggie responded, with a southern drawl, "I do have a client," she got a little mad and said, "But I ain't one of those prostitutes you always talkin' about. I'm a female escort."

"Yes, madam, you interested in these costumes?"

"Do you have one of these for a man? He's two inches shorter than me, and how would I look in this one?"

"Yes, we do, and you would look great in that. Anything else?"

"Yes, I'll take one of those leather whips and three pairs of those. I got a good credit card."

"Very well. Looks like your client is going to have a good time."

Maggie faked a little mad again. "Yep, he's havin' the time of his life. Remember, I ain't one of those whores that come in here. I'm a professional."

He checked her out, gave her the card and then said, "Here is your card back. Thank you so much, Bonnie."

Maggie pulled the VW out of the lot of the "Politician's Sex Shop". She had a quick stop at the Home Depot, then she could head home to get ready for her first week at her new job.

✧

Her first days of work were fairly routine. Maggie followed the Congressman around for the most part, taking dictation, attending meetings, and attending a few lunches with supporters. She was put on a committee to shore up Representative Baker's reelection campaign.

The days were busy and long. Maggie had to wait until after hours to really get to use the staff computers. Once she got the opportunity, they were extremely easy for her to hack. She waited until Thursday after hours to start her real work.

She found a Molly Jones from New Orleans, Louisiana. She was able to replace every record of her as Molly Jones with this other Molly. Fingerprints, identification cards, employment records, purchases, and anything else she could find on her as Molly Jones was wiped out and replaced with the Louisiana Molly, 103 years old.

She lifted the Fournier mugshot photo from the library and scanned it into her computer. She attached it to a timed e-mail along with a brief description of Fournier/Baker's former activities. On Saturday morning, *The Washington Post* would learn some interesting tidbits about the Congressman.

Friday arrived, and the workday was busy. Maggie knew today was the day. She had to wait until near quitting time for it to happen, but she knew that Congressman Baker was staying in Washington for the weekend.

At precisely 8:00 p.m. Maggie got the call to meet Representative Baker in his office.

She entered and saw him sitting behind his large desk. He stood up and said, "Welcome, Molly. You had a very productive and successful first week."

"Oh, thank you," Maggie said with a big smile. "All I want to do is help you run this country here in our nation's capital."

"I have one more thing for you to do today. Will you please file these papers for me? They go in the bottom drawer of that file cabinet."

As Maggie bent over to file, she felt his hands on her butt cheeks.

Maggie stood up. "Congressman, what are you doing?"

Baker put his arm around her waist and lifted his head to kiss her neck from behind. He quietly said, "Come on Molly, you said you liked to play the game. Let's go get a drink then head over to your place."

"Oh Congressman, I am so embarrassed. I do like the games, but I have a better idea."

The congressman moved his hand up and squeezed Maggie's breast.

Maggie pushed him away. "No, no. not here, not good. Why do we need to go for a drink? Yes, yes, I have the best gin and tonic at my home."

"Great. Let's go."

"And Congressman,"

"Call me Bob."

"Bob, I love the game, but I like the game a little kinky."

"You don't seem like the kinky type, but I love kinky. How kinky?"

Maggie said with her nasally voice, "Yes, yes, I am so embarrassed. I am into S&M."

"What's S&M?"

"You don't know? You dress up in costumes. One is the slave, and one is the master. I love to be the master."

Baker said, "Let's get out of here. I'll meet you there."

Maggie met the Congressman at her front door. She handed him a stiff gin and tonic.

"Thank you." he said.

"Yes, yes. I made it just how you like it, and I have many more. Let us go down into the basement. That is where all the fun is."

She led him downstairs. The basement was dimly lit with a few old pieces of furniture and boxes. Baker didn't notice that Maggie had installed a large hook on the wall along with two pairs of handcuffs, fastened about two feet away from the hook on each side.

Maggie took Baker in her arms and gave him a long passionate kiss.

The Congressman said, "This is just what I need, a stiff gin and a hot woman."

Maggie responded, "Yes, yes, and now it is time for the game." She handed him a plastic bag. "Take off your clothes and get into this costume. I am going to go upstairs to get into mine."

Baker took off his clothes and put on the costume. There were two black leather straps crisscrossing around his hairy chest and another two crisscrossing around his waist. Over his groin was a black leather cup covering his privates. There was something that looked like a dog collar, black leather with big silver rhinestones.

Baker heard someone coming down the stairs.

"Bad Congressman! Bad Congressman!" Maggie's nasally voice sang out. Baker heard something that sounded like a cracking whip.

Maggie continued snapping the whip as she slowly walked down the stairs. "Bad Congressman!"

She wore a bikini top that consisted of three black leather straps across her breast and a black bikini bottom. She had nylon stockings covering her long slender legs with four-inch black high-heeled shoes. Her La Belle Époque wig was covered by a black scarf. Maggie still wore the thick rimmed brown glasses.

When she saw Baker in his costume, she did all she could to keep from laughing. She approached him slowly and stuck her tongue in his mouth.

She sternly said, "I am master. You are slave. You have to do as I say."

He timidly said, "Sure."

Maggie cracked the whip loudly. "Get on the stool!"

She had a two-foot stool placed right in front of the hook. The Congressman stepped on it.

"Now give me your hand." Maggie took his right hand and fastened one of the cuffs around it.

"Now the other one."

Baker said, "Molly this is getting a little weird. Why don't we just go to your bedroom?"

Maggie pulled down the straps over her right breast exposing it. "If you want this, give me your hand."

Baker obliged as Maggie cuffed his other hand. She used the last pair of hand shackles to cuff his two ankles together. Finally, she reached behind him and securely wrapped the straps of his costume around the hook. She stepped back and threw the whip at his feet, then wrapped the end of the whip five times around a leg of the stool. She yanked the whip hard, pulling the stool out from under his feet sending it flying across the basement.

Maggie looked at the Congressman with his arms spread out and his feet dangling in the air a foot and a half above the ground. She took a headband with a large red rubber ball fastened to it, put the band around his head and stuffed the ball into his mouth.

Maggie started laughing. "This is too funny. I need to take a picture."

She snapped a few flash pictures, then took the headband and ball off Bob.

THE ANGEL AND THE AMAZING LIFE OF MAGGIE LOVE

"What the hell are you doing?" Baker yelled with rage. "Get me down at once. I'm a United States Congressman."

Maggie ditched the nasal accent. "Sorry Bob, I can't do that."

"What is this, blackmail? What happened to your voice?"

Maggie kicked off the high-heel shoes. She removed the nylon stockings and leather bikini, staying naked for just a few seconds. Nearby, she had a long white dress with patches of marble red splashed throughout. She put the dress on over her head. It fell to her ankles.

"Bob, you get the rare chance to meet someone few people have met."

"What! There is someone else here? Help, help!" Baker yelled. "There's a crazy woman down here!"

"No one can hear you down here, Bob."

Maggie took off the scarf and the wig throwing them aside. She took off the wig cap letting her light brown hair with natural streaks of silver hang down to her shoulders, she used a handkerchief to wipe the red lipstick off her mouth and took off the glasses. Finally, she used her fingers to take out the brown contact lenses.

Maggie looked at the dangling Congressman. "Like I said Bob, you get to meet someone." She stared at Baker making sure her green eyes sparkled right through him. "You get to meet Maggie Love."

⁓

Maggie went upstairs to pack a few things and to keep Bob Fournier dangling for about a half an hour. She could tell his screams for help were getting louder and more frantic. It was time to return. This time she would be concealing something under her dress.

When the Congressman saw Maggie coming down the stairs he said, "Okay, Molly. You got me. I'll pay you whatever you want. Just get me down."

"I told you; my name is Maggie. You think I want money? Can't let you down Bob. I need information first. You know, men are so stupid. I thought I might have to drug you to get you into this wonderful position. All I had to do is show you a little titty, and it's a done deal."

"What information? I am a US Congressman. You want to extort me for information just because you have an unflattering picture of me?"

Maggie started laughing loudly. "Who would want to see a picture of you looking like this? You look so Congressional." Maggie pulled up her dress and took her 38 special Smith and Wesson revolver out of a leg holster. "You got it all wrong, Bob. If you don't give me the information I want, I'm just going to shoot you."

"You're crazy, you can't kill a United States Congressman. They will find you. I have people that will find you, Molly."

"How can they find a person that doesn't exist? I was born in a basement, probably not much different than this one. I never went to school. I never get sick. I just do not exist. And one more thing, call me Molly one more time, and I am going to shoot you."

The angry Representative said, "Okay, get me down, and I'll tell you anything."

"Can't do it Bob,"

"Alright, what do you want?"

Maggie said with a smile, "Isn't it great when an employee and her boss can have a nice little chat like this?"

"What do you want?"

"Tell me what you know about the Mestiño Society."

"Mol... I mean Maggie, what is this about? That was a long time ago."

Maggie cocked the hammer of the pistol and pointed it at Baker.

He said with a shaky voice, "Okay, it was set up as a nonprofit to help horses, but they didn't help a one. The board of directors collected millions from horse lovers all over the world. When they had enough millions, they made the organization disappear. The only expense they had was a very small ranch in Illinois. That was set up just to fool the suckers they scammed."

"Who are these board of directors?"

"The chairman, the guy who set this whole scam up was a New Yorker named Clyde Snell. He took his so-called profits to New York and made millions more in real estate. I sat on the board. And there was a French connection."

"A French connection? Isn't that kind of cliché? Like the movie?"

"I didn't know much about them. They seldom came around. There were three of them. French guys named Dubois. I know they got a lot of money. That's all I know, I swear. Now, let me down."

"Not yet, Sherlock. What do you know about Alison and Rob McLander?"

"I don't know them."

Maggie stood close to Baker, took the collar around his neck and tightened it one notch. Baker started to struggle and pull on the cuffs to try to break free.

Maggie asked, "Are you a gasper, Bob? This collar is designed for them."

The struggling man said, "That's making it very hard to breath."

"Alison and Rob McLander?"

"Okay."

Maggie released some of the presser from the collar.

"He was an accountant, and she worked in marketing for the society. When they were hired, they didn't know it was a scam."

"I guess they found out," Maggie said.

"I guess so. Rob McLander embezzled a couple of million, then they disappeared. That's all I know."

Maggie got up and moved her hands close to the collar.

Baker said, "All right, all right, Snell and the French connection wanted the money back and wanted them dead. Snell caught on to the embezzlement. We confronted them, and that crazy Alison woman shot one of the brothers before they escaped. Snell and the Dubois brothers promised me a big bonus if I found them. They would not let up. Me and my boys chased them for eight years. Then we finally found them."

"You killed them?"

"No, here's the thing, when we finally found them, they were already dead."

"So, you got your bonus. That was enough money for you to create a new identity and a successful run for Congress."

"Yes, but I didn't kill them."

"I know who killed them."

"Who?"

"I did. Well to be exact, my mother killed my father. I killed my mother."

"Wait," the hanging man said. "They didn't have any kids."

"I told you Bob. I was born in a basement. I don't exist."

"I do remember my boys said there was a dollhouse and some toys around in that basement."

"I was only seven when I shot my mom, and I used this gun. My mom trained me for years to do it. I was so short then." Maggie knelt down in front of Baker with the gun in both hands.

"Like this tall. I pointed the gun at her head like this. Then I fired."

A terrified Baker started to cry, "Please don't kill me. I've told you all you wanted to know."

Maggie got up off her knees. "I'm not going to kill you, Bob. I asked you if you were a gasper."

Baker stopped crying for a moment. "What is a gasper?"

"I worked in the adult entertainment industry for a year or so. You pick up this stuff. There's a perversion called erotic asphyxiation. That's where you choke yourself, and right before you die, you orgasm, then you release the presser from around your neck."

"I'm not a gasper. Maggie, please let me go now."

"I never tried it. I heard it was a little dangerous. What the hell, let's give it a try."

Maggie reached for the collar and tightened it two notches. Baker immediately started to gasp and cough. His face turned beet red.

The gasping continued as Maggie said, "Don't worry, Bob. I'm going to release it before you die."

Soon the Congressman's eyes started to bulge out of his head. His body started shaking wildly, then it all stopped. His body went limp.

"Oh, I'm so sorry, Bob. I didn't release it soon enough. Oh well, I told you it was a little dangerous."

Maggie left Bob Fournier and all the sex equipment in the basement and walked up the stairs. Before she got to the top, she talked back at the dead man, "Bob, I was right. You are a gasper. If you think they are going to find me through the house rental, I didn't rent the house. It was rented by a southern gal named Bonnie Dickerson. She has a reputation around these parts as a girl that can show a man a good time for a fair price. She's a real professional. The cops are going to think that she was here tonight, to help you with your perversion."

⁓⌇⁓

Maggie took her suitcase and put it in the trunk of her car. She opened the garage and backed the car out. There was a man standing by the sidewalk. She got out. James Cannon put his arms around Maggie and gave her a long kiss.

After about ten seconds, Maggie pulled away. "James, what the hell are you doing here?"

"I had to see you again Molly," He looked at her closely. "What happened to you? You look even more beautiful. I don't see how a woman could be more beautiful. Your voice is different."

"James, you promised."

"I didn't promise not to see you."

Maggie whispered, "James, go home. I must leave. In a day or so cops will be crawling around all over this place."

"Where are you going?"

Maggie got back into the car, looked out the window and said, "I can't tell you."

She pulled the car into the street, put it in reverse and came back. She looked James right in the eye. "If you ever want to see me again, solve the riddle."

Maggie drove off.

⁂

Maggie never cried but as she drove, she felt an unusual tear in her right eye.

"What's the matter Maggie, feeling a little emotion?" the Inspector asked.

A startled Maggie looked to her right. She almost drove the car into the curb.

"Oh, it's you. You know you almost had me fooled this time. For the most part, I thought I was living that for the first time."

The Inspector had on his fedora and trench coat. "I found out a while back that nobody can fool you. Do you repent for killing that Congressman?"

"Be serious Inspector. That sleaze bag basically killed my parents. He tried to fuck me after my first week at work."

"You're not the prosecutor, judge, and jury on this. Do you repent?"

"Yes, I am, and no I don't."

"Do you repent for killing James Cannon?"

"Now, you're wacky. I didn't kill James. I just saw him."

The Inspector tried to explain, "Sometimes a woman can kill a man by breaking his heart. We have millions of cases."

"And that's murder?"

"In a few cases, yes."

"I have you this time. I didn't kill James, and the sleaze bag was a gasper. It was an accident. Am I dead Inspector? You can't be an Angel. Are you the Grim Reaper?"

"Yes on question one, no on question two. Maggie. Do you repent?"

Maggie looked at him and firmly said, "No."

When she looked back at the road there was a tree coming right at her. She hit the tree, throwing her over the steering wheel and through the windshield. The Inspector got out and looked at the bleeding woman lying on the hood of the car.

"I'm getting too old for this job."

Maggie's mind exploded.

VI. THE ANGEL

I AM STARTING TO DOUBT WHETHER MAGGIE LOVE IS A TRUE PSYCHO-path. I don't think she is that self-centered. Maybe she feels some emotion, even if it is ever so slight. After the killing of her mother, there was little love and an almost complete absence of guilt during her life. But during her last examination, I was starting to learn that there is a method to her madness.

I had to meet with The Consul again. This time it was not to reprehend me but to advise me. Why did they do this? I have been an Inspector for over two thousand years. Since the Consul never takes human form, I must revert back into a Bliss Being. This transformation is very difficult to accomplish because it requires much time and energy. I'm getting so tired of this job. After two thousand years, maybe it's time for a change.

The two male Beings still wanted to see her terminated. The three female Beings wanted to see more. Then came all the advice. The meeting only lasted four milliseconds. It seemed like days.

After five inspections, this Maggie Love has stressed me into indulging in some of your worldly cravings. They are sometimes referred to as cancer sticks. I think I'm puffing down about a pack a day now.

I knew what I had to find out next, and I certainly did not need the Consul's advice. I had to examine an earlier part of her life. I needed to learn how the wicked tortures of puberty affected Maggie Love.

6. In Her Teens

MAGGIE WOKE UP.

The spinning and dizziness were intense. Everything was spinning so fast that Maggie fell to the floor. She got up and as the room started spinning faster, she fell again.

"Get up, Maggie!" she heard a concerned female voice. "Are you okay? You fell out of bed."

Maggie tried to move closer to where the voice was coming from. She started to crawl.

"Maggie! Let me help you up."

The spinning in the room started to subside and Maggie got up and tried to walk. The pain in her head was extreme. She tried to be strong and started to walk towards a fuzzy image of a woman walking towards her. She staggered as she walked, and the image of the woman started to come into focus.

"Mom?" Maggie asked as she got close. She fell into her arms as one more giant spin shook the room.

"Maggie, are you alright?" Sally Love asked. "Are you having another bad period?"

"No, it's not that, Mom. I just got so dizzy. My head is killing me."

"Adolescence does the strangest things to a girl. Get back in bed and lay down. I'll get you some hot tea."

Maggie looked around the bedroom as memories started to come back into her mind. She was lying in a double bed with a pink canopy over the top. There was a white desk with a matching dresser. She knew she was in an apartment in Southern California.

There was a full-length mirror on the wall. She got out of bed and took a look at herself. Her hair was light brown, almost blond, with streaks of silver. She had green eyes, and her skin was an amber tan. She felt very tall. When she looked at herself again, she thought, "Am I a California girl?"

Soon, Sally came back in with a steaming cup of tea, "Maggie, get back in bed until this dizziness passes."

"I think I'm okay now, Mom," The memories were coming back, but she was still a little confused. "How old am I?"

"You'd better not be taking any drugs or smoking any of that weed. We just talked about this the other day," Sally said.

"No, Mom, no way. I'm not doing that stuff. I am just confused because of this terrible headache."

"In two weeks, you're going to be sixteen. I wanted to throw you a little sweet sixteen party, but you want to go back there, to that place."

Maggie knew she was talking about. She had to go back to Colorado. She quickly did the math and realized the year was 1971.

"You know I don't have many friends Mom, and maybe it's my birthday in two weeks. We really don't know."

Sally hugged her foster daughter. "That's what the phony papers say. August 27 is as good a day as any. Why don't you let me register you at the high school? You're so smart, and no doubt you'd be the most popular girl in school."

"Mom, you know it would be a waste of time. I could teach all the teachers. I like the home-schooling thing."

"I'm not home schooling you, you are home schooling me," Sally said. She looked at Maggie. "You're getting so tall. You are at least two inches taller than me. That means you are five foot nine already."

"Silvia is coming over today. It's Saturday and we want to go to the beach, and you know I'm driving." Maggie said.

"Shouldn't you let Silvia drive? She's seventeen and has a license. Maggie, you're only fifteen."

"That's not going to happen, Mom. That girl drives like a maniac, and I have been driving for over two years now. Nobody has stopped me yet."

"True. I'm glad you can spend time with Silvia. You two are such good friends."

Maggie replied, "It's better to have one true friend than hundreds of so-called friends."

VI. THE ANGEL • 6. In Her Teens

Maggie loved to drive. She took Sally to work at the diner, then she got the car for the rest of the day. She wanted to go to a beach in Orange County. It was almost two hours away, but Maggie didn't care. The two girls were going south on Interstate 405 in the Love family's green Volkswagen Bug.

"Why don't we just go to Santa Monica? It's way closer," Silvia asked.

Although Maggie's friend Silvia was almost two years older, she was now three inches shorter. Silvia was all blond with long straight hair. Her tan was as dark as Maggie's.

"Balboa Beach is way less crowded. I hear the guys aren't as horny. All they want to do is surf."

The two lived in the same apartment complex in Reseda. Like Maggie, Silvia didn't go to high school either. She dropped out at the beginning of the year.

"Maybe I could use a horny guy right about now," Silvia said.

"No way girl. You know how stupid and abusive they are. Remember your Dad."

"I know, and now Mom says I have to get a job. It's not easy being a single mom with three kids. Dad's never coming back."

Maggie asked, "When does he get out of prison?"

"He got twenty years. He might get out earlier for good behavior."

"After the way he abused you and your Mom, the rapist got off easy."

They found an uncrowded spot just to the south of Balboa Pier. Maggie spread out a large beach blanket and the two girls took off their beach sarongs, kicked off the flip flops, and put on dark glasses as they prepared for an afternoon of sunbathing. The soft clouded marine layer was starting to burn off, letting the sun slowly creep in. As it warmed up, the sound of the crashing waves seemed to increase. More people crept in also, ruining some of the solitude the girls were feeling.

"You look extra hot in that yellow bikini, girl," Silvia said.

"Mom says yellow is my color. Looks like green is yours."

"You got that right." Then Silvia asked. "Do you want any suntan lotion?"

"You know that's greasy kid's stuff. I don't need it."

"I just don't want you to get skin cancer Maggie Love, if that's your name."

"Why wouldn't it be? It might be Doeskin or even McLander. Something tells me I'm going to have lots of names during my life."

"I'm just sticking with Silvia Johnstone. One name is more than I can handle."

Silvia stood up and spread her arms out as if to hug the ocean. "Maggie, do you know what I love best when the marine layer burns off?"

"I suppose it's the way the sun glistens off the ocean."

"No girl. It's the sky. It's so wonderful here. No smog, no clouds, just endless blue, blue sky. Maybe I should become a pilot, so I could fly through the sky."

"Not on my watch. I have seen you drive. If you got a pilot's license, there wouldn't be a bird in the sky left alive."

"Maggie, there's a couple of older guys over there by the pier. I think they want us to come over."

Maggie lowered her sunglasses to see. "They look like creeps to me, especially that fat one."

"I'm going to check it out. I'm getting a little bored. Come with me?"

"Nope. If you're bored, go swimming."

"Come on Maggie, you know I can't swim."

Maggie could swim. She walked towards the waves and entered the sea. When a big wave approached, she dove into it, then swam past the breakers. She treaded water for a while when she noticed Silvia was waving at her. She slowly swam towards the sand.

When she returned, she grabbed her towel and started to dry off. "What did they want?"

"I'm so excited. They offered me a job. They seemed to be even more interested in you."

"A job? Doing what?" Maggie asked.

"He wasn't too specific. He just said big money and a few hours a week. I have an interview next Thursday. They want me to bring you along also. I told them we were both eighteen."

"Not going, Silvia. You know me better than that. Where is this interview?"

"It's a house in San Fernando. He wrote the address on the back of this card."

Silvia handed Maggie the card. She looked at the address, then flipped it over. The front of the card read, "Gene Raymond Productions."

The ride home on that Saturday was easy, until they got near Los Angeles International airport. Then the L.A. traffic attacked them with a vengeance.

As the cars slowed down, Maggie asked. "You're not going to do this interview, are you?"

"I'm thinking about it, and you know I need a job. They offered me a job, and there aren't that many jobs around right now."

"Silvia, don't do it. I can smell a creep a mile away."

"I'll think about it less if you come with me to Josh Miller's party next Saturday."

Maggie said, "I don't drink beer, I don't do drugs, and I won't know anybody. Why would I want to go?"

"You need to get out," Silvia replied. "All you do is read, go to the library, hang out with me, and then you read some more. Maybe you'll meet a guy you like."

"Odds are hovering around zero percent that that's going to happen. Okay, I'll go with you, but just for an hour."

"Great. Josh's parents are away for the weekend. He lives only ten minutes from us. I'll drive you."

"I want to be alive when we get there. I'll drive."

※

Maggie spent the week planning the trip to Colorado. Driving was the best choice. She figured if they only stopped for gas, they could make it in fifteen hours. She still had to convince Sally to come with her. It would be easier if she had a guardian, and by Thursday night, she thought she had her convinced to come along. They sat in the living room with the TV tuned to *The Flip Wilson Show*.

"Mom, if we leave a week from Tuesday, we will arrive very late Wednesday. I'll make an appointment at 11:00 a.m. Thursday morning. I'll be sixteen by then."

"Why do we need to go to Colorado?" Sally asked. "You know I'm scared to go anywhere near that place."

"We're not going anywhere near Byers. The place I need to go to is in downtown Denver."

"I've spent the last nine years trying to forget about that night, and now you're bringing it back."

Maggie reassured her, "This is going to be fun. It's a road-trip like the one we took nine years ago, in the opposite direction."

"I said I'd go and if we're only stopping for gas. I'll pack some road-trip lunches."

"Thanks Mom. I really need to do this. If it's any consolation, it should be much warmer than it was that freezing night so long ago."

The dial-up phone, hanging on the wall near the kitchen suddenly rang. Sally got up to answer it.

"Maggie, it's Silvia."

Maggie took the phone..

"Hey girl." Maggie said into the phone.

"Guess what?" Silvia said back.

"You went to the interview."

"Hey, you're not supposed to guess it right."

"So, what happened?" Maggie asked.

"I'll tell you at the party."

"I'm not going to the party. You went to the interview, so I'm not going."

"Then you will never find out."

"I have to wait until Saturday?"

"If I tell you before, you won't go to the party."

"See you Saturday. Goodbye Silvia."

⌘

The Saturday night weather was perfect. As the sun went down, the Southern California temperature was sixty-eight degrees, and the girls decided to walk to the party.

"Now remember Silvia, my name is Debbie," Maggie told her sternly.

"Debbie Love?"

"No! No last name. I don't need a last name at this party, just Debbie."

VI. THE ANGEL • 6. In Her Teens

Maggie wore dark blue denim Levi's and a plain yellow t-shirt. Silvia had on light-brown Levi's with a green-flowered blouse.

"What's with the granny-bun hairstyle and the glasses?" Silvia asked.

"I don't want to attract any attention."

"You can hide behind a bad hairdo and corny glasses, but you can never hide that bod."

As the night got darker, few stars were visible; Los Angeles smog was shielding the stars from their view.

"Are you going to tell me about the interview?" Maggie asked.

"Are you going to go home after I tell you?"

"I said I was going to this party, so I'm going."

"They hired me on the spot, and I got a hundred dollars cash. They want me to go back next Monday." Silvia was almost gushing.

"Cool, but what did you do Silvia?"

"I just did a couple of scenes. I was there for only four hours. They had a big camera and spotlights and everything."

"Scenes, what scenes?"

"Don't tell my Mom. I did some sex scenes. I did one with a guy and one with a girl. My head is all messed up because of my abusive dad, so that's my excuse for doing this."

"A messed-up head is why you need to get out now." Maggie got in front of her friend and put her hands firmly on Silvia's arms. "You need to stop this before it's too late."

Silvia said back, "I'm going next week. Gene seems so nice, and they promised me two hundred this time. Now you promise you won't tell anybody."

Maggie said reluctantly, "I promise, but you have to stop."

The two started walking towards a blue two-story house. Maggie would handle Silvia later. She had to get through this night first. Everything in her mind told her to turn around and go home. The déjà vu in her head told her she had to go in. She had to enter the party.

There was so little light in the house that Maggie had to wait a minute for her eyes to adjust to the dark. There was a quadraphonic sound system blaring out Three Dog Night's, "Mama Told Me Not to Come," from four speakers placed in the four corners of the living room. There seemed to be about twenty people in the room and more hanging elsewhere. They were all high schoolers and most of them had a beer. The smell of marijuana filled the room, coming from some unknown location.

The music was so loud Maggie had to yell at the top of her voice into Silvia's ear, "Let's go in the back! There are a couple of chairs!"

"What!" Silvia yelled back.

Maggie took her hand and led her through the crowd to the back. The two sat down and Maggie looked at her watch, it read 9:05.

She yelled to Silvia, "Only fifty-five minutes to go!"

During the next thirty minutes a few guys tried to talk to Maggie. Maggie acted like she couldn't hear them, and they soon went away. Silvia was screaming back and forth with some guy when a six-foot three-inch young man stood before them. He had stringy long brown hair covering his ears and his jaw seemed too big for his face. He was trying to flash a look that said that he was in charge.

He yelled at Silvia, "Hello, Silvia! Who's your friend?"

"What?" Silvia yelled

"Who's your… wait a minute!" He turned to a shorter blond boy, "Turn down the music! Put on something softer! Nobody can talk!"

The blond boy yelled, "What?"

He put his mouth close to the blond boy's ear. "Put on something softer!"

Soon, the hard rock-and-roll stopped, giving the guests a few seconds of ear-pleasing silence. It was replaced by Stevie Wonder's "If You Really Love Me."

The young man said, "That's better. I asked you Silvia, who's your friend?"

Silvia stood up, "Josh this is Mag—I mean Debbie. Debbie, Josh. He's the quarterback on the football team."

"Silvia doesn't know much about football. I'm the wide receiver. This year will be my third year as a starter," Josh said proudly.

Maggie stood up to shake his hand. "Thanks for having us."

Josh checked out Maggie's body. "Not bad. I haven't seen you at school, Debbie. Are you a dropout like Silvia?"

Maggie said, "no," while Silvia said, "yes."

"You know I've been charging everyone two dollars a beer. But for you two ladies, it's on the house. What can I get you?"

"I'll take a beer," Silvia said.

VI. THE ANGEL • 6. In Her Teens

Maggie replied, "Just a soda for me."

A boy started talking to Silvia while Maggie sat alone. Soon Josh came back with a can of Budweiser and plastic glass filled with soda.

"Drink up. It's hot in here with all these people," Josh said as he handed them their drinks.

Maggie felt unusually thirsty, and she drank almost all of it. Silvia sipped her beer and continued to talk to the guy.

"Debbie, do you want to come up to my room to see my trophies?" Josh asked.

"I'd rather not."

"Come on, don't be scared. Bill will come with us."

He grabbed Maggie's hand and led her up the stairs. Once in the room Maggie felt dizzy. She went to the bed and sat down.

She tried to say, "did you drug…," then her head fell back on the bed.

Josh looked at Bill. "Get out of here. Bill, I like that song. Play it again and louder so I can hear it up here." After he left, Josh locked the door.

Maggie tried to move her arms, but nothing moved. She tried to talk but there was no sound coming from her voice. She felt someone taking off her pants, then there were violent kisses all over her face. Maggie could barely see but she felt the penetration. The rape lasted for over five minutes.

The young man got off her and she heard him say, "You're a pretty good whore. I'll have Bill take both your drunk ass and your friend's drunk ass home. Get dressed."

Maggie used all the power her mind could muster to try to overcome the effects of the drug. She sat up and her first instinct was to go home, get her gun, and come back and shoot him. She thought it through, however, and quickly formulated a plan.

She timidly said, "Oh I'm so sorry Josh. Silvia and I took some bad downers. They really kicked my ass."

"You should be sorry. You're lucky I don't spit on you."

Maggie put on her pants. Her mind was rapidly defeating the drug. She said, "I thought I could make it up to you. Maybe we could go out?"

"Are you going to put out?" Josh asked.

"Yes, I'll show you the best good time."

"Okay, my girlfriend is on vacation for another week. I'll pick you up at eight on Monday at the gas station on the corner. I don't want anyone to see me with a whore like you."

"I'm so happy, Josh. I don't want anyone to see us either."

Maggie didn't let Bill take them home. It was obvious that Silvia got the same treatment as she did. She was fast asleep on the floor and Maggie waited until she was up and able to walk, then she slowly guided her out of the house and onto the sidewalk.

"What the hell happened? I just had one beer and I passed out," Silvia said as she hung on to Maggie.

"Whatever he put in your beer, he put in my soda."

"What happened to you? I saw you go upstairs with him. Did he hurt you? Did he try anything?"

"It was rough, but nothing I couldn't handle."

"What are we going to do?"

"You're going to do nothing. I have a little work to do over the next few days."

Maggie got up early on Sunday. She didn't have time to worry or sulk about the rape. She had to stay positive to accomplish all she needed to do. But first, she got her lavender vanity box out from under her bed. She opened it with a four-digit combination. Inside, underneath her revolver, was the envelope her mother gave her nine years ago. The note inside was in her mother's handwriting. There was an address to a bank in downtown Denver. Her mother wrote below the address, "Go to this bank when you are sixteen. Give them this key." Maggie looked at the small golden key. Soon she would find out what secrets it would unlock.

There was a knock at the door. Maggie put the key and envelope back in the box and said, "Come in, Mom."

Sally entered her room, "Do you want breakfast? I'm off this week because of our big trip. You know I am getting a little excited about it. It's going to be fun."

"I'll take a little breakfast, and it is going to be fun. It's good you're not working; I need the car for the next couple of days. So much to do you know."

"We are only staying one night. We'll get a hotel when we get there."

"Right, Mom where are the tools?" Maggie asked.

"There are a few under the kitchen sink. Why do you need tools?"

"Oh, I've got some tinkering to do today."

After breakfast, Maggie took some screwdrivers and a butter knife out to the Volkswagen. She sat in the passenger side. She used the tools and knife to take the buckle apart on the lap seat belt. She knew what to do as she put it back together with one extra piece. Then she tested her theory. It worked perfectly. She next worked on the shoulder belt with the same positive results. She practiced a few more times until she could pull off the task in a just a couple of minutes.

She got in the driver's side and sped off. She needed to go to the gas station and then a quick trip to the music store. She wanted to buy a new cassette.

On Monday evening, Sally came into Maggie's room.

"You're here?" She asked, "Where's the car?"

"Hi Mom. Silvia has it. She needed to run a few errands."

"You let the girl that can't drive use our car?"

"She's getting better. I've been giving her a few lessons."

"Are you having dinner here? I'm making pork chops."

"No, way," Maggie said with a smile. "I'm going to take a walk, then meet Silvia. She's going to pick me up out front. We're going to grab some Chinese."

"Are you going to order it in Chinese?"

"I would, but I don't think they speak Mandarin at this place. It's some other dialect."

Sally smiled. "You're the only person in the world that learns an entire language just because you like the food."

Maggie arrived at the gas station a little early. She didn't worry that he would stand her up. He was a guy, and she offered him sex. Sure enough, at 7:55 pm, a yellow and brown Ford Pinto pulled into the station. Josh Wilson was driving. When he stopped, Maggie got in the passenger seat.

Maggie tried to keep her voice soft and sexy. "Hello Josh. I am so happy you came."

"Okay, it's Debbie, right? Where do you want to go?"

THE ANGEL AND THE AMAZING LIFE OF MAGGIE LOVE

"I have a secret place where I take all my boyfriends. Get on Topanga Canyon and go south. It is in the hills about twelve miles away. This is such a cool car."

"Yeah, my old man got it for me brand-new when we took league. I caught a touchdown pass in the last minute that won the game."

"You're so good Josh," Maggie tried to sound sexier. "You don't even have to wear seat belts."

"Hell no. If I don't make the NFL, I'm going to join NASCAR because I'm a great driver. You know you are kind of pretty when you take off those glasses."

"Thanks Josh. Maybe we can do this every time your girlfriend goes away."

They got off the highway and headed towards Topanga State Park. Soon they were going up a dark winding road. They passed a few swanky houses, then the paved road turned into dirt.

"When are we going to get there?" Josh asked.

"It's just a little further. The road ends soon, and we will come to a dirt roundabout. That's where we park."

When they got to the roundabout Josh said, "There's a car here. I thought you said this was a secret place?"

"Oh, that car is always here. I think it's a wreck. Don't park too close to it; there might be a homeless living in there."

When they parked, Maggie put her arms around Josh and gave him a long passionate kiss. She smacked her lips softly and said, "Take your pants down Josh. My mouth is watering for it."

Josh did exactly that, then Maggie said, "It will be much better if you're strapped in."

She reached across him and grabbed the lap belt. She buckled him in and then did the same thing with the shoulder harness. Maggie quickly took the keys out of the ignition. She opened her door and walked over towards her waiting Volkswagen.

"Where are you going?" Josh asked.

"I'll be back in a jiffy."

She opened the door of her car then turned on her cassette player full blast. It was playing the song, "If You Really Love Me." Maggie headed back to the Pinto, walking in rhythm to the music, and carrying a plastic two-gallon jug filled with a clear liquid. In the other hand she had a large plastic glass.

With the passenger door still open, she crouched down and said, "Do you like this song, Josh? I think I remember hearing it the other night. The night you raped me."

Josh tried to undo the seat belt. He struggled and said, "There's something wrong with this thing. It won't open."

"You know Josh, you shouldn't leave your car unlocked at night. It makes it much easier if someone wants to tinker with it. I like to tinker."

With Stevie Wonder singing in the background Josh said, "When I get out of here, I'm going to kill you."

Maggie replied, "You got it all wrong Josh. I am going to kill you."

Maggie took the jug and filled the glass with liquid.

"Look at this glass, Josh. It looks just like the one you gave me the other night. The night you raped me."

She threw the liquid at Josh's face.

He yelled in a panic, "Ow! That stings! What is this? Gasoline? Are you crazy?"

"Yes Josh. I get crazy when a guy rapes me. You're a big boy. You need more glasses."

She threw two more glasses of gasoline at him. As he fought to try to get off the seat belts, Maggie reached into her back pocket and took out a box of stick matches.

She took one out of the box and showed it to Josh. "I'm going to make sure you never rape a girl again." She struck the match against the box, and it lit with a small flare.

Josh was crying, "Debbie don't do this. I'm sorry. Debbie, please don't do this."

"Here's the thing, Josh. My name's not Debbie."

She flicked the match at Josh and as he ignited, she firmly said, "My name is Maggie Love!"

Josh started screaming and patting his body with his hands to try to put out the fire. Maggie went around to the front of the car and opened the hood. She poured the rest of the gas over the engine, making sure to get plenty near the fuel line. She put the jug and glass on the side of the engine and lit another match. She dropped it on the gas. The engine erupted in flame, then she closed the hood.

"Another thing Josh," Maggie said over his screaming, "These Pintos have a bad reputation of blowing up. Too bad yours is going to blow up also."

The screams got louder as the fire started to burn deeper into Josh's skin. The panic got so loud that Maggie wanted to cover her ears. Then the squealing screams suddenly stopped.

Maggie walked briskly to her car. "One more thing Josh. With your pants down, the cops are going to think you were out here jerking off."

She got into her car and started to drive away. Through the rear-view mirror, she saw the fiery explosion. When the fire reached the fuel tank, it blew the trunk hood ten feet into the air.

"It's for you." Sally handed Maggie the phone.

Maggie and Sally got a good night's sleep. The plan was to leave around 9:00 a.m., drive until around midnight, get a room in Colorado, then be at the bank at 11:00 a.m. the following morning. They packed an overnight bag and some lunches. Maggie made sure she had her vanity box in the car.

Maggie said into the phone, "Hello girl, what's up?"

Silvia answered, "I'm scared Maggie."

"You went to that job? I told you to stay away."

"I went. When I got there, Gene was in one of the rooms screaming and yelling. He was throwing chairs. It looked like he beat one of the girls. I think they found out I'm not eighteen."

"What did you do?"

"I got scared and left. I hope they don't come and hurt me."

"I don't think they'll do that."

"He was saying they could all go to jail for statutory rape."

"I'm going to take this quick trip to Colorado. When I get back. I'll think of something."

"I'm just going to stay inside."

"Good plan. I'll see you in a couple of days. Stay safe."

VI. THE ANGEL • 6. In Her Teens

The setting sun was behind them as they drove east on Interstate 70. They could see the Rocky Mountains in the distance. The Utah desert landscape was amazing. The mountain sculptures to the north looked like God had a wonderful day when he crafted them, with multitudes of reds and burnt orange in shapes no human could ever design.

"Are you going to finally tell me why you need to go to Colorado on your sixteenth birthday?" Sally asked her daughter.

Maggie was driving, "Get my vanity box. It is on the back seat. The combination is 4-4-4-8."

Sally opened it and looked inside. "Why did you need to bring this gun?"

"You never know when you might need it. There's an envelope underneath. Read the note." While Sally read, Maggie continued, "My first Mom gave it to me before she died. Before I shot her."

"I never believed that story, Maggie. So, what does this key open?"

"I have no idea. I've been curious for nine years. It looks like we are going to hit the mountains soon."

"You better pull over and let me drive. You've been going for like nine hours straight,"

"Okay, Mom. Did you bring me some reading material?"

"On the floor in the back, both the Los Angeles Times and the Herald Examiner. There's a flashlight too. It's starting to get dark."

The magnificent mountain view was now blocked by darkness. Maggie was looking at the newspapers with a flashlight shining on page after page while Sally drove carefully over the massive mountain range.

When they got close to Vail, Colorado, Sally asked, "Do you want to get a hotel in Vail? We can stop at the same place we did last time."

"No, please no. I think that place was haunted or something. Let's drive over the mountain and get a place in Denver, close to the bank. Good thing we brought lots of lunch. I am sure all the Chinese places are going to be closed by now."

They found a cheap hotel in Denver, and it was 1:00 a.m. when they went to bed. Sally turned off the light. "I'm exhausted. That was a wild ride."

Maggie turned to her. "You know Mom, I was kind of thinking it might be a good time to move. I haven't been a good girl over the past couple of days."

Sally said with alarm, "Move? Why? What did you do Maggie Love?"

"I did what any red-blooded American girl would do. I defended my honor. There might be bullying for what I did. It would be good to get me away."

"I know there's no way in hell you're afraid of any bullies. Where should we move to smarty pants?"

"Mexico."

"Mexico? What am I going to do there? Do they have diners?"

Maggie said quickly, "I've been reading about this up-and-coming resort town in the southern Baja Peninsula. It's called Cabo San Lucas. Only a few hotels there now, but many more coming in the very near future. I always wanted to learn Spanish."

"If you could learn French and Chinese, you can learn Spanish. Let's talk about it later. Time for bed now. I hope I can sleep; I'm going to be wondering all night what we are going to find at that bank tomorrow."

As they waited in the bank lobby, Maggie said, "Use the ID I gave you."

Sally answered back, "Every time I think of that name, I shiver. It scares me."

Soon, a man in a dark suit with a long mustache and wire glasses came up to them. He had a finicky voice. "Hello, are you Mrs. Hatfield and Maggie Doeskin?"

"Yes, we are." Maggie said.

"I'm Mr. Filches, the bank Manager. We have an unusual case here. I have special instructions. This box was started nine years ago, and they paid for twelve years in advance. A woman named Jane Doeskin paid."

"My parents are deceased now," Maggie said.

"I'm so sorry, Maggie. I've also been instructed that Maggie must be sixteen, and I need the proper documentation."

Sally handed him the papers.

He said, "I see Mrs. Hatfield that you are Maggie's legal guardian, and it says here that today is Maggie's sixteenth birthday. Happy Birthday from everyone here at The Bank of Denver."

"Thank you, sir," Maggie said.

He led them to a vault and started turning the combination wheel until the large door opened. Inside was a room with golden boxes lining the walls on all three sides. The small ones were on the top. The bigger boxes lined the bottom.

"Yours is number 902. Can I see your key please?"

Maggie handed him the golden key. He crouched down to a bottom box and put it in the keyhole. Then he put his own key in the second keyhole, and it opened. He took out the large box that was inside and lifted it up.

"This is a heavy one," he said as he led them to a private room. The room had a high table and a couple of stools. He placed the box on the table."

As he left, he said, "Take all the time you need. Just ring the bell when you are finished."

"This is it, Mom," Maggie said.

"This is so exciting."

Maggie slowly lifted the lid and looked inside. The first thing she saw were some coin rolls. She took one out and opened it. The coin was about the size of a silver dollar. She inspected it, then handed it to Sally.

"It says fifty Pesos on it. That's Mexican. That's not very much."

"Mom, it's dated 1947. I think each one is about a troy ounce of gold. Each roll has twenty coins. How many are there?"

Sally said, "Let's count them."

They took them out and put them groups of ten. Maggie counted twenty groups.

"Jesus, Mom. It's not even legal to own gold in the United States."

"It isn't?"

"No, not since 1934. We have two hundred rolls of twenty. That is four thousand coins. Gold was trading yesterday at forty-four dollars and sixty cents. That means we have $178,400 dollars here.

Sally almost fainted. "How do you know that?"

"I read the paper yesterday, remember?"

"There's more inside," Sally said.

Maggie reached in and took out some certificates. She looked at one, then handed it to Sally.

"What's this? International Business Machines Corporation? It says one-hundred shares. It has Maggie Doeskin as owner."

"That's IBM, a big business machine company. Count them, Mom."

Sally counted the papers. "Looks like there are two hundred of them."

"I'm not so good at stocks, but I think IBM closed around eight bucks yesterday. We have twenty thousand shares. That's about $160,000 dollars."

"Maggie, there's a brown paper bag in there."

Maggie opened the bag. Inside were neatly wrapped stacks of one hundred-dollar bills. Maggie counted the stacks. "There are forty stacks of hundreds in here. Each stack has a hundred. Mom, that's $400,000 dollars. All together we have a total of $738,400 dollars."

Sally hung on to the table to try to keep from falling over. "Maggie, what are we going to do?"

"Let's take five stacks of hundreds and five rolls of coins. We'll leave the rest here until I figure this out. We have three more years of rent on the box."

"Maggie, there's one more thing in there." Sally showed her daughter a small white envelope. All it said was a hand-written MAGGIE on the front.

"Let's take that too," Maggie said.

They were getting close to home, and Sally was driving the last leg on Interstate 15 south. They were passing the Las Vegas hotels and casinos to their left.

"Do you want to stop and put a couple thousand on a hand of blackjack?" Maggie asked.

"No. We can use that money to get caught up on my bills."

"Sorry Mom. We need to use that money to move to Mexico. Some people might come around to ask questions."

"What did you do, Maggie?"

"I told you; I was defending my honor. I'm thinking it might be wise to leave tomorrow."

"We just drove two thousand miles. Now, you want to drive two thousand more. What am I going to do there? I'll lose my job at the diner. You're just going to leave Silvia?"

"Silvia can come with us. Mom, we have enough money in this car for us to buy a restaurant and a house in Mexico."

"My own restaurant. Wow I can make some of my country specialties. Okay, we can go. I'll call it a vacation."

"Mom, if you own a restaurant in Mexico, you might want to learn how to make a taco."

"Of course. Do we need passports?"

"No, we'll just drive across the border. I'll tell them we are going shopping."

"Maggie, you should probably open that note that was in the box."

She took the envelope and opened it. "There is an address to a bank in Albuquerque, New Mexico. There's another key in here."

"Really?"

Maggie didn't tell her there was a note written below the address. In capital letters it read, "I LOVE YOU, MAGGIE."

Maggie didn't cry.

*

Maggie and Sally got back to the apartment after 10:00 p.m..

"Let's pack tomorrow and leave about nine in the morning. I'm going to call Silvia and tell her what's going on."

Maggie dialed the phone. "Is Silvia there?"

She listened for a while then dropped the phone receiver. The long-curled cord made it bounce back up a few times after it hit the floor. Maggie stood there wide-eyed with a blank stare.

"Maggie, are you alright?" Sally asked.

Her voice was choked up. "Silvia's dead."

"No, Maggie, it can't be." She hugged her daughter.

Maggie didn't hug back. "They found her in the bathroom at a park tonight. The cops say it was a drug overdose or a suicide. It wasn't. I know she would never do that."

"Think of all the wonderful things you two did together. Remember her love."

Maggie finally hugged her Mom back. "She loved the sky Mom. Silvia loved the sky."

Maggie retreated to her room and closed the door. She lay down on her bed and looked at the ceiling. Then she felt something present.

"Not now Inspector. I just lost my best friend," she said.

Inspector Lawrence sat down at the bottom of her bed. "I'm sorry Maggie, but this is not about that. Do you repent for the killing of Josh Wilson?"

Maggie got up and sat next to the Inspector. "No, the fucking bastard raped me. I don't think this is about repenting at all. This is to show me what a failure I am. I supposedly have this amazing mind, and I couldn't save Silvia." Maggie's eyes were red and teary.

The Inspector took a puff off his cigarette, "You had nothing to do with her death. Do you repent for killing Josh?"

"No, I don't. I could have put off the Colorado trip for a few days and been here when she needed me. I can tell you one thing; those porno guys are going to get theirs."

"Knowing you, I'm positive that will happen. Please, Maggie repent."

"I think I remember telling you this before, "Cram it up your ass. What are going to do now? Throw me out of a flying airplane? Are you going to cut my head off?"

"There's no need for that anymore." He reached up and touched Maggie's forehead.

Maggie's mind exploded.

VII. THE ANGEL

There is a place I have to go when I meet the Consul. They call this place "The Chambers." Imagine an area that is confined but has no end. There are no walls, no ceiling, and no floors. It is surrounded by a dense fog of energy with a random bright spark exploding all around. There are no energy blasts in the center of The Chambers. Only the Consul members are there, floating in a ring. In the middle of that ring would be the Being that is being subjected to an interview. Again, I had to convert from human form back into a Bliss Being. I was in the center of that ring to listen to their arguments and absorb their advice.

The Male Beings argued that if Maggie were a male, she would have already been terminated. They had almost convinced one of the Female members who was leaning towards termination. All the Male members needed was one more vote, and it would be all over for Maggie Love. This leaning female member asked if there was a time in her life when she was happy and content. I had no idea. Every exam so far always revealed murder and death, but her last exam did reveal some affection towards her friend and foster mother. That was my new assignment: to find a slightly better Maggie Love. I knew this was possible, but in order to save her, I had to find a gentler and kinder Maggie Love.

7. In Her Forties

MAGGIE WOKE UP.

She was surrounded by a thick haze that was both inside her head and outside of her body. The ground in front of her was higher than where she was, then it violently dropped below her. Up and down it went as the hazy landscape began swinging back and forth. Maggie felt she was running through a cloud. She abruptly stopped; the dizziness was forcing her to her knees. There was the feeling of cool sand beneath her fingers. A wave of cold water came across her hands and legs wetting them briefly, then returning to wherever it came from. She looked to her left as the dizzy fog started to clear. The was a mountain on the other side of a bay of blue water. To the left of that, the mountain was gone and there was a view of endless ocean. A brilliant dot of red sun was rising out of the sea.

A bigger wave of water splashed all over her. This time, the force of the receding water wanted to take her with it.

A young Hispanic man was jogging toward her. He spoke Spanish, *"Are you alright, Ma'am? It looked like you fell down."*

"I'm fine thank you. just a little dizzy." Maggie's Spanish was perfect.

He offered his hand and helped her up.

Maggie said in Spanish, *"My head is killing me, and I got so dizzy. Do you mind if I ask, where we are?"*

"Okay, I get it ma'am. You had too much Mexican tequila last night. That happens a lot to the white girls that come to visit us. This is my home, and you are in Cabo San Lucas, Mexico."

Memories started to come back to her. She looked away from the water. She knew she didn't have far to go. She walked along the shore towards a boat-filled marina, and when she saw a place that had a huge canopy painted with wild colorful dragons, she was positive that this was her destination. In the back was a bar filled with colorful bottles of liquor the stretched across the entire back of the canopy. The sign over the roof was large, in red and green letters. It read, "Sara's Mexican Heat."

A young Hispanic woman was setting up chairs around one of the fifty tables under the canopy. She saw Maggie and said, "Hello, Big Sis. Mom wants to know if you could help out behind the bar tonight. A guy called in sick. You've been back only one day, and we are already putting you to work."

Maggie's sister Laura Love-Hernandez looked in perfect shape for a twenty-five-year-old. Her amber skin and short black hair was the perfect look for this part of Baja California.

Maggie gave Laura a slight hug. "Okay Little Sis, I'll help. It's been a while since I tended bar. Where's Mom?"

Maggie knew where she was. The déjà vu in her head told her. She felt that she had lived this before.

"She's at the hotel. She's trying to settle a little dispute there."

Maggie walked behind the restaurant and up twelve concrete steps until she reached an iron gate. She opened it with a key and walked by a large pool surrounded by tall palm trees and banana plants. There were guests sitting around the pool in blue lounge chairs. The beautiful view over the restaurant showed the multi-shaded rocky Mount Solmar and the bay in front of it. A few patrons were ordering morning drinks at a coconut leaf-covered bar to her right.

The Hotel Excelsior had four stories and sixty-two rooms. Each one had a balcony facing the bay behind Madano Beach. The entry doors were all in the back of the hotel. Maggie walked the flowery, yellow-painted halls until she found Sally Love in the back. She was with a man wearing a beige-colored sport coat. There were two security guards with her.

Maggie approached the four. "What's up Mom?" She kissed her mom on the cheek.

"Oh, we got some squatters locked in this room," Sally Love said in English.

Sally had short grey hair and black-rimmed glasses. She wore a beige-colored business suit that matched the man's coat. The clothes looked like they might be a little uncomfortable in Baja's ninety-degree heat. The stress of running a restaurant and hotel kept the fifty-eight-year-old Sally in very good shape.

The man in the sport coat said in Spanish, "*Yes, they paid for one night. Now they have been in there for two, and they won't come out.*"

Maggie kissed the man on the cheek. "*Hello Papa.*"

Hector Hernandez was a short man with a big smile. His dark-black greasy hair shined in the morning sun.

Maggie said, "*Let me handle this. You two have more important things to worry about.*"

"*I'm so happy you're back. You can make life a little easier around here,*" Hector said with a smile.

One of the guards unlocked the door with a master key. He opened it only to be stopped by the chain door-guard. He pushed his shoulder against the door a few times until the chain broke free.

Maggie entered the room and closed the door. Sitting on one of the double beds was a skinny young Mexican man and woman. On the floor were what looked like a two-year-old boy and a four-year-old girl who had been playing with some stones. Now, their wide eyes stared at Maggie.

"*So, you don't have any money to pay for the room?*" Maggie asked in Spanish.

The young man said, "*Please Ma'am, can we stay just one more night? It is so hard to sleep on the beach. We have to go get cardboard boxes in town, and we try to make a shelter.*"

Maggie asked, "*Why don't you work? You look like a strong young man.*"

"*I can only move my right arm like this.*" He moved his bent arm back and forth parallel to his belly. "*No one will hire me.*"

"*You are hurt and handicapped? How did that happen?*"

"*I was with some bad guys a long time ago. We were trying to smuggle some cocaine into the United States. The Federales caught us, and they did not even bother to arrest us. They just cut into our shoulders with a sharp knife, leaving our right arms useless.*"

Maggie said, "*Don't mess with the Federales. Does your left-hand work?*"

"*Yes. Very well. You learn how to get by when you only have one, you know.*"

"*And what about you, Ma'am?*"

The woman said, "*I would work, but I have the babies. No one to watch them.*"

"*What are your names?*" Maggie stayed relaxed but stern.

"I am Cecelia, and this is my husband, Juan."

Maggie sat down on the bed across from the couple. "Here is what I am going to do." She reached into her jogging shorts and took out some pesos. She handed the money to the man. "There is enough here for a few nights at a place outside of town. Go there after you two are done today."

"Done with what?" Juan asked.

"I'm giving you both jobs. You start right now."

Cecelia said, "Thank you so much Miss …?"

"Barbara," Maggie said.

She continued. "Thank you so much Miss Barbara, but I still have the babies."

"We have a Nana here who takes care of a few kids. She can watch them until you get back on your feet."

Maggie left the room. Sally and Hector were waiting outside. "There're going to leave now. I gave them jobs. I'll have Felipe set them up. She can help clean the rooms, but he's a bigger problem, He's a little disabled."

Sally asked, "How disabled?"

"He can't use his right arm."

"I bet he could wash windows with one hand. Don't you agree, Maggie? Whoops I mean Barbara," Hector replied.

Maggie said, "Yes, Papa, I am Barbara and I have a better idea. Let's train him to tend bar, so I don't have to. That would be something, a one-armed bartender."

Sally said, "I hope you doing this doesn't make it to the streets. We will have every homeless in Cabo banging on our door."

⁕

Maggie's next plan was to go to her villa, get some rest, then come back in the evening to help out at the bar. She would take a taxi to her condo and pick up some Chinese food on the way. As she was walking out the back of the hotel, she passed the Nana's room. Through the window she saw Nana Susana, a totting little girl, and a ten-year-old boy. The boy was dressed in blue pants, a white shirt, and a red necktie. That was his school uniform. Maggie did not go in.

⁕

VII. THE ANGEL • 7. In Her Forties

"I need to know how much money you make," the woman sitting across from James Cannon asked. She had dark skin and big brown eyes. Her voice was determined.

James said, "What? This is our first date."

The restaurant just outside of Washington DC was fairly crowded on this cool May night. James decided to try dating again after seemingly hundreds of failed attempts.

"I know that, James," she said. "This is DC. There is no time. Everyone's busy, and a girl doesn't have time to waste dating a guy who's not an earner."

"I don't think this is going to work out."

She said right back, "Thank you James for saying that now. We won't waste any more time."

The woman grabbed her bag, got up, and walked out of the restaurant.

James threw a few dollars on the table to pay for the wine and followed her out. He decided to walk the few miles to his house.

As he walked, he prayed he wouldn't have that reoccurring dream again tonight. The dream where there is a long kiss, and then she drives away. He promised himself that he would never look at that silly riddle again. That was just Molly's way of torturing him.

As he walked, he noticed a local church he passed was having a Mayflower Festival.

"A Mayflower festival in May," he thought.

He decided to get a coffee before his return home for a lonely night alone. He entered "The Perk It Up" coffee house and was greeted by the usual, "May I help you?"

James said, "Hi Cindy. You always say may I help you, even though you know I'm going to have a medium mocha."

"Hi James," The barista said. "The owner wants us to say, "may I help you" to every customer that comes in. So, I say, may I help you."

"Yes, you may. I'll have a medium mocha."

When he got to his small house, he went into his office and fired up his computer. He looked at the news, read some e-mails, and then he broke his own promise. He took out the riddle that was printed out on a piece of paper.

"Who am I? I might be Molly. Never ask why. Drop the why. Gee, join the Army and add everything. E is for everything. I can never feel love.

It is impossible for me to feel love because I am love. Now, you need to learn Spanish."

As he read it, he said to himself, "This is just gibberish. Maybe I should go to the Mayflower Festival. I could meet a nice church girl."

He looked at it again. "No, is it that simple? She did not say I might be Molly. She said I MAY BE MOLLY.

He had tried thousands of ways to convert the name Molly, and nothing ever worked.

"Is it May? Never ask why. Drop the why. Then you have M-A. Gee? That is M-A-G. Join the Army. If you join the Army, you become a G.I. Now I have M-A-G-G-I. Add everything. E is for everything. M-A-G-G-I-E. She said "I can never feel love. It is impossible for me to feel love, because I am Love." She is love. Her name is MAGGIE LOVE!"

James was now talking quite loudly to himself, "Why would I need to learn Spanish? Is she in a place where they speak Spanish? I'll try Mexico."

James spent the night searching the internet for a Maggie Love in Mexico. He wished he had learned Spanish. His search was constantly being slowed by bad translations.

He searched the birth record, death records, police records, anything he could find. No Maggie Love. He searched real estate records and found that a Sally Love leased a property in Southern Baja California. It was a restaurant named Sara's. He checked the net and to his amazement, they had a web site.

"Pretty good site. They must have someone with technical skills there. Could it be Molly?"

There was a phone number. He dialed it but added the fifty-two-country code first. There were four long monotone beeps before a female voice said in Spanish, "*Sara's Mexican Heat. How can I help you?*"

James said in English, "Can I talk to Maggie Love please?"

The voice on the phone switched to English and yelled, "As anyone seen Maggie? Whoops. I'm sorry sir, there is no Maggie Love here." She hung up.

James put down the phone, He stood up, then dropped to his knees. He raised his arms high in the air and screamed, "I found her!"

VII. THE ANGEL • 7. In Her Forties

Maggie and Sally were sitting in Sally's office behind the front desk of the hotel. Maggie sat on the other side of her mother's desk.

"Mom, it's time to sell this place," Maggie said.

"What are Hector and I going to do if we sell it?"

"Try a nice retirement. You can move back to the US. I hear there is some great farm properties in Byers, Colorado."

"Very funny, Maggie. This is your place, and you can sell it when you want."

"Within a year, and thanks for helping out with the muchacho." Maggie got up and kissed Sally on the cheek.

"What choice do I have? You're never here. Have you spent five minutes with him since you got back?"

"At least six," Maggie said dryly.

"One other thing, Maggie. It was a busy night last week and a guy speaking English called the restaurant and asked for Maggie Love. Laura blurted out a "Where's Maggie?". Then she told him no Maggie here and hung up. She feels just awful about it."

Maggie said with no emotion, "Oh, he finally found me. It took him long enough."

"Who found you?"

"Expect a visitor soon. A guy from Washington DC."

─────

James got out of the cab at the Cabo San Lucas Marina. He paid the driver with dollars then started the short walk to Madano Beach. It was just past 10:00 a.m. and people were already starting to enjoy the water, the jet skis, and the kayaks. He saw a woman over the water being tugged by a motorboat with a red and yellow parachute behind keeping her far above the Sea of Cortez.

He kept walking north keeping his eye on the bars and shops to his left. When he saw the sign Sara's Mexican Heat, he approached it slowly.

A Mexican man greeted him when he got close. "Welcome to Sara's, Senoir. Come in, we have the finest breakfast in all of Cabo."

He showed him to a table under the canopy. Within seconds he had a glass of ice water with a waitress handing him a menu.

James said to the waitress, "Can I talk to Maggie Love please?"

The waitress said back, "Sorry Senoir, no Maggie Love here."

James felt a powerful presence from behind him, a presence he had not felt in years. And then he heard the voice. "Took you long enough James."

James turned around and looked up. He fell out of his chair and onto the sandy floor.

Maggie stood tall. Her hair was bleached blond with what looked like hundreds of tight braids hanging down six inches below her shoulders. Her hair seemed to get darker as it made its way down her face. Each thin braid was tied with a yellow ribbon on the end. Below she wore a yellow and green flowered beach sarong with a matching bikini top. The forty-three-year-old looked closer to twenty-eight. She took off her big round dark glasses, making sure her green eyes shined.

James said from the floor, "Molly?"

"No, James, Molly is dead." Maggie offered her hand to help him up. "Let's go to the bar and have a drink."

They sat at the long bar and were greeted by a skinny young Mexican bar tender. He spoke in Spanish, *"Good morning, Miss Barbara. What can I get for you and your friend?"*

"Yes Juan, get us each a Tequila Sunrise and make mine a virgin."

Soon Juan was tossing ice cubes into the air one at a time. He caught them in a tall glass. He filled the glasses with orange juice, poured a shot of tequila in one, and topped each one off with red grenadine and a garnish of orange slice and maraschino cherry.

"He only uses one hand," James observed.

"Yeah, he had some issues with the Mexican authorities a few years back. I think he is faster than most of the two-handed bar tenders we have here."

James asked, "Isn't it a little early for me to be drinking, Maggie?"

"Shush James. This is Cabo and here you can drink any time you want. When we are alone, my name is Maggie. Everywhere else I'm Barbara."

"Why all the mystery, Barbara?" James said mockingly.

Maggie answered, "You look good James. Looks like you gained a few pounds?"

"I'm an IT specialist now. All I do is sit at a computer, not enough exercise."

"Good thing you're wearing sneakers and shorts. You do need some exercise, so let's go to the beach."

When they left the restaurant, James took Maggie's hand.

Maggie used her nasally Molly Jones voice, "No, no. No holding hands. Not my boyfriend."

James dropped her hand.

"Just kidding, James. Let's go to the other side of the bay to Mount Solmar."

When they got to the nearby shore, Maggie waved to a boat. The captain of the small water taxi guided his glass bottom boat close to the shore, then he got out to try to hold it steady as the two got in.

"That's a beautiful view of that mountain," James said as they motored across the Sea of Cortez.

"Wait till you see the view from the top. We are going to hike it."

They walked for a while until they came to a rusty green gate across from a naval base and near a dog rescue kennel. Maggie gave the man that owed the kennel a donation of a handful of pesos, and he opened the gate for them. The path ahead started off fairly flat. It got steeper and rockier the further they went.

Maggie was almost but-not-quite jogging, and James started to lag behind. "Maggie, I'm not sure I can make it, this is getting too steep."

Maggie turned around, "Come on James. It's only a couple of miles. The view at the top is amazing. How old are you anyway?"

Breathing heavily, he said, "I'm forty-four and way out of shape."

"This will help you get back in shape." Maggie turned around and proceeded up the trail and soon she came to the toughest part of the hike. She had to grab the rocks and use them for stairs until she reached the summit. There was a nine-foot-tall white cross planted there covered in graffiti. She touched the cross with her left hand and swung herself around it 180 degrees, so she was facing James. He was fifty yards behind her.

She had time to enjoy the view. She saw a point called Land's End that was to the south where the Sea of Cortez meets the Pacific Ocean. From the top of the hill, she could see all of Cabo San Lucas.

James was getting closer, and Maggie noticed he had a small camera and was taking pictures of her. She immediately climbed down to his level.

"Give me the camera, James," she said with anger in her eyes.

James handed her the camera. Maggie opened the back of it and pulled out the long coil of film exposing it to the light.

"What are you doing? I just took a couple of pictures of you."

"It's not your fault. You didn't know. Take pictures of the landscape but never take pictures of Maggie Love."

"Why the hell not? You looked so beautiful up there."

"Never take pictures of me James, because I don't exist."

⁓⁓⁓

They walked down a steep, rocky trail until they came to a beach. With the Pacific to their right, Maggie took James's hand as they walked to the south.

"So, what have you been doing for ten years, and why did it take you so long?"

"That riddle drove me crazy. I was ready to go nuts. I tried to forget you, I even tried dating."

"How did that work out?"

"The last date I had lasted ten minutes."

"The riddle wasn't that hard James."

He looked at her and tried to explain, "I'm not stupid, but you never wrote it down. I got one word wrong."

Maggie changed the subject. "This is the Pacific side; it is called Divorce Beach. Do you know why?"

"No."

"If you throw your spouse in there, the current is so strong that it will pull them out to sea, and they are never seen again. Now we are coming to Lover's Beach. That is to our left on the Sea of Cortez side and straight ahead is the Arc of Los Cabos."

"Maggie, it's so amazing here. I'm in the most beautiful place in the world with the most beautiful woman in the world."

"Shut up James," Maggie said, then asked a question. "Which one do you pick, Divorce Beach or Lover's?"

"I think I'll take Lover's."

"Let's take a water taxi back to the hotel."

"Hotel?"

The boat started to pitch back and forth as they approached the opposite shore, and Maggie asked, "What was the scene like after I left ten years ago?"

"It was crazy. The Capital Police and the DC cops were everywhere. They blocked off the street for days. A Congressman Baker was dead inside your house."

Maggie knew the answer, but she asked anyway, "So what was the conclusion of their investigation?"

"First, they said it was a murder. They changed that and said it was an assisted suicide, but then they finally concluded that it was a weird sex act gone wrong."

When the captain of the taxi got close to shore, James got out first.

Maggie said, "I think number one is the right answer."

James put both his hands on Maggie's waist to help her out of the boat. "Why do you say that?"

Maggie jumped out of the taxi. As her feet hit the watery shore, she looked at James and said, "because I killed him."

◈

Maggie opened the gate, and they entered the pool area. They sat down at a table for two near the bar.

"This is a beautiful hotel. Look at that view of Mount Solmar. I can't believe I hiked over it," James said.

Maggie asked, "Where are you staying, James?"

"I got a hotel a couple of miles inland. It was cheap."

A pool boy brought them two more Tequila Sunrises, one virgin.

"Check out of there a little later. I can give you two choices. We can set you up here, or you can stay with me. I have a villa in a gated community nearby."

"It's wonderful here, but I think I'll go with choice number two."

"Okay, maybe we can watch movie like *Dirty Dancing*. Let's go meet some people. Bring your drink. I am sure you will need it."

Sally and Hector were both sitting behind their desks when Maggie and James entered the office.

Maggie introduced them. "Hello Mom, Papa. This is James Cannon. James, this is Sally and Hector Hernandez. They run the hotel."

Hector stood up with a big smile, shook his hand, and said in Spanish, *"Oh, you must be the American that called last week."*

James looked at Maggie, "What did he say?"

"I told you to learn Spanish, James. He said you called last week."

Sally got up and shook his hand. "Nice to meet you James, and welcome to Cabo."

James said, "This place is amazing. It must be great to own a resort like this."

"He doesn't know?" Sally asked. "Does he know who you are?"

"He knows I'm Maggie. Not much else."

"One more thing, Maggie. Bruce was in here a few minutes ago. He wants to know if you'll come to his soccer game tomorrow," Sally said.

"We will go see him next," Maggie said as they left the office.

Sally said, "And James, we don't own this place. Maggie does."

Maggie looked in the window of Nana Susana's room. The boy was sitting behind a desk doing homework. Maggie entered the room.

She said with little emotion. "James, this is Bruce. In Spanish we pronounce it Bru-che."

James crouched down near the boy. "How old are you Brucie? I hear you like to play soccer. I used to love to play when I was young."

He answered, "I'm ten. We call it football here. Mom, who is this man? I think I like him."

James turned around and looked at Maggie. "Mom?"

Maggie said, "Good thing you like him, Bruce. His name is James. He is your father."

The crouching James lost his balance and fell to the floor.

―――

Maggie was walking briskly near the shore on Medina Beach. James was trying to keep up.

James angrily asked her for the third time, "I've had a son for ten years, but you never told me? Maggie, you knew where I was."

She answered back, "My name is Barbara."

"Knock it off. I could have helped you. I would have been with you through everything."

"If you had solved the riddle sooner, you would have." Maggie started jogging.

James kept up. "Don't give me this riddle shit. Why didn't you tell me?"

Maggie stopped. "You're right, James. I should have told you, but not for those reasons. I should have told you because I'm the worst mother in the world. I leave all the time. Bruce doesn't even live with me because Mom and Hector are raising him. Maybe that's why I didn't tell you. I'm the worst. I don't have the mother's gene."

James was trying to hold back the tears. "You can't be that bad."

Maggie handed him a piece of paper. "Here's what we do. Check out of your hotel and take a taxi to this address. We will talk more tonight. And I am that bad."

⁂

"Do you want to stay here a while, James?" Maggie asked has she filled his wine glass.

Maggie's Villa was small and sparsely decorated but it had two bedrooms, a kitchenet, and two full baths.

"I have to get back to work in a week," James said.

"You don't. You can work here and since you made such a big deal about not knowing you had a son, maybe you should try to get to know him a little."

"What would I do here? Do you need an IT guy?"

"I need a hospitality guy. You can be an assistant manager. I'll bet you will look great in one of those beige suits."

"I don't know anything about hospitality, and why doesn't Bruce live here with you? You have plenty of room."

"You will learn. You're a smart guy, I think. One thing you need to learn about Maggie Love is there is never much time. I may leave at any minute."

"You want me to stay, and you are going to leave?"

"I'm willing to try the domestic thing for one month. If it works, I'll stay longer."

James got worried. "Everything is happening too fast. I need it to slow down so I can think. If it works out, would you consider marriage?"

"No way in hell is that going to happen. Drink some more wine, James." Maggie filled his glass again.

James said, "Just one more thing. You implied on the beach that you killed that congressman. You were just joking, right?"

"Of course not James. I would never joke about a thing like that. Have some more wine, then let's go to bed."

They were trying to cram ten years of love making into one night. Rolling across the bed and changing positions every fifteen minutes did not exhaust them. It was three in the morning before sleep finally came. There was no time to watch *Dirty Dancing*.

~

James came in through the front door of the Villa. It had been one week since he started his new job at the hotel. The time was 7:15 p.m., and James was wearing a beige sport coat that had "Hotel Excelsior" printed on the lapel.

Young Bruce came from his room to greet him. "Hi Dad. You worked late today."

"I didn't think the hotel business could be this crazy. It seemed so glamorous looking at it from the outside. It's not. Seems like you have to put out a fire every ten minutes. Where's your mom?"

"I think she went out jogging. She never says where she's going. She just leaves. She did say she would bring back some dinner."

They sat down on the couch and James asked, "It's been a week now since you moved in with us. How do you like it?"

"It's okay. The Chinese food gets a little old. I complained, so she said she would bring Mexican tonight."

"I wish I knew her better. She seems very distant. I can't tell if she is happy or not." James seemed worried.

Bruce said, "She is always in her own world. She just reads and runs and reads some more."

"Well, we have to do everything we can to try to make her happy."

Maggie came through the front door carrying two bags of food. She spoke Spanish, *"I got this at Sara's. We got tacos, chalupas, rice, and beans."*

Bruce answered also in Spanish, *"Sounds great. Did you bring hot sauce?"*

"Yes, we must keep up with the Spanish, so your Papa learns it."

James said, "I can't understand much of this. I did understand taco."

While in bed that night, Maggie read a book written in French, *Le Tour du Monde en 80 Jours* by Jules Verne.

"Bruce seems to be a really smart kid," James said.

"I think he is smarter than most of his teachers. Did you know I never went to school? And that I was born in a basement?"

"Then how did you learn so much? You seem to know everything, and you speak three languages."

"I speak four. Mandarin Chinese is my fourth, and I'm learning Arabic."

"You were born in a basement? Oh, and by the way, since I wasn't there, how was Bruce's birth?"

"It was rough. But nothing I couldn't handle."

"We've been together a week now. I want you to stay. I've heard you disappear a lot."

"I said I'd try it for a month, and I will."

"I love you, Maggie. Is it possible, you love me just a little?"

"Shut up, James. You know what I'm going to say."

"I know. It is impossible for you to feel love because you are Love."

They were passionate for most of the night, for the seventh night in a row.

It was now their thirtieth day together. The days always seemed the same in Cabo, ninety- plus degrees and sunny. When the sun went down it cooled off quickly. The breeze coming from the sea helped air condition the sandy beach. Maggie and James walked barefoot in the cool sand by the shore.

"I want you to stay. Bruce wants you to stay. Your Mom and Hector want you to stay. So, are you going to stay?"

"I haven't made up my mind yet," Maggie said coldly.

"I can think of a million reasons for you to stay. I can't think of one reason why you should leave."

Maggie stopped and faced James, "Look at me James, look in my eyes. Do you want to hear one reason I need to leave? I will give you one reason. I'm a God damn serial killer, James!"

"What are talking about?"

"You should take Bruce, go to the airport, and fly as far away from me as possible. Take Mom, Hector, and Laura too. I don't deserve to be close to anyone. I told you about the Congressman. It's not just the Congressman. If you count my Mom, I've killed seven people and I'm not done yet."

"Maggie, you're delusional. You did not kill your Mom. I was just working with her today."

"Sally is my foster Mom. I shot my real Mom in the head when I was seven years old. She trained me to do it. Have you ever shot your mom in the head, James? Do you know what that can do to a person?"

James tried to calm down. "I got to think this through. It can't be true, and even if it is, I don't care about your past. I love you now. If you were in trouble, why didn't you go to the authorities?"

Maggie hugged James closely and tightly. She whispered in his ear, "James, James, the authorities? I've killed seven people. And besides, do you know why I don't need the authorities, James? It's because I am Maggie Love."

James knew it would be their last night together for a while. The passionate lovemaking went on well past two in the morning. James got up and turned on the light. He looked at the beautiful woman sleeping naked on the bed. He did not want to sleep, and he was afraid of the morning. He knew when he woke up, poof—she would be gone.

She had an early flight out of Cabo. Maggie was wearing a long yellow and green flowered dress. Her braids were gone, leaving her hair a sandy blond. She was greeted at the ticket counter by a cheerful young ticket agent. Maggie showed the young lady her identification.

The agent said in English, "Hello Miss Hamilton."

Maggie said, "You can call me Anita."

"Okay Anita. We have you flying into Houston, then a plane change there and off to La Guardia in New York City."

Maggie checked her bag and made it to the escalator. Going through security she felt this was all wrong. There was someone behind her. She didn't turn around. She just said, "Hello Grimmy."

The Inspector caught up with Maggie. "You know, I told you I'm not the Grim Reaper."

"I know, so you're my Guardian Angel. Grimmy sounds much better."

"Funny. Maggie you're developing quite a fan base where I come from."

"Where's that?"

"This place is called the Bliss; there are Beings from all over time and space taking an interest in you, even the members of the Consul."

"What's a Consul?"

"Oh, they're these five bigshots that kind of run the place."

"Can I tell you something, Inspector? You need to get a new fashion consultant. It is 1999 in the middle of summer in Cabo San Lucas, and you're dressed like Humphry Bogart."

VII. THE ANGEL • 7. In Her Forties

"You remember everything now?" the Inspector asked.

"I always figure it out in the end. It just came to me when I felt your presence."

"See, that's never happened before in the history of these examinations. That's one of the reasons your fan base is growing. Beings think you are something special."

"I don't want fans Inspector, and I got you this time. I haven't killed anyone during this exam."

"I told you about the broken heart. How do you think James is feeling right now?"

"James will be fine. He has a son now, and he can work in Cabo or take Bruce anyplace he wants."

"He wants to be with you, Maggie."

"Let's speed up this process. Instead of asking me three times to repent, let me just say this: cram it up the asses of the all the Consul members," Maggie laughed.

"We don't have asses in the Bliss."

The Inspector waved his hands in front of her eyes.

Maggie's mind exploded.

VIII. THE ANGEL

I ONCE TOLD YOU, WHAT IS OBVIOUS HERE IN THE BLISS IS WAY OVER THE heads of the living bodies on the Below World. Maggie was starting to prove the point of her being different to me again. She always seemed to have a plan, and she was always two steps ahead of her adversaries. Now I am almost sure that she was not a total psychopath.

During Maggie's last examination, I tried another one of your worldly vices. This is the one you call bourbon. I have seen this alcohol drink destroy many a life during my angelic career, but I also heard that a taste of this concoction can relieve stress. So, I sat at that beach front bar in Cabo and had a few shots. This is what Maggie Love has done to me, and if it goes on much longer, I may become a regular at *Sara's Mexican Heat*.

I know Maggie made it through another examination, but The Consul wants more. As far as I know, eight exams are an all-time record. I cannot tell if the Consul is being wishy-washy and indecisive or if they are just enjoying the Maggie show. Under my protest, they gave me precise instructions on what to do next. After this, I am positive that this will be my last case. This has never been tried before, and I'm not sure if I can pull it off, but I must try. I would never quit an examination of a soul before it was resolved, so here goes nothing, or will I find something? They want me to examine the conception of Maggie Love.

8. In Her Zeros

MAGGIE WOKE UP.

She felt warmth. She saw nothing, heard nothing, and thought nothing. She just felt warmth. It was all around her, entering her body. She felt a surrounding energy, filling her body with life. There was no dizziness, just a feeling of contentment. There were no memories pounding into her head. She did not have any. Maggie didn't want to leave this place. She knew she was well-protected.

Alison McLander got off her exhausted husband's naked body. She stood up and put on a white bathrobe she had nearby and walked towards the bathroom. When she got to the door, her knees buckled beneath her causing her to crouch down on one of them.

"Are you alright, Alison?" Rob McLander asked. "Did you slip?"

"No, I didn't slip. It felt like a thousand volts of electricity just went through me."

"Did you get shocked?"

"No, I never felt anything like it. I know I'm preg...."

"No Allison, when did you find out?" Her husband asked.

He put on his bathrobe and went to her to help her up.

"I found out just now, when I fell." Allison struggled to get up.

Rob put his arms around her and hugged her tight. "I know you felt something, but you need to see a doctor and take the tests."

"No Rob," Alison said quickly. "We don't need a doctor now. I am positive I am pregnant. There is one more thing I'm positive about, Rob. It's a girl."

The next morning was bright in Phoenix. The Arizona sun shined through the window of their small one-bedroom apartment, lighting up the room much earlier than Alison wanted. She got out of bed.

Rob McLander was already up, dressed, and ready for work. He wore a thick-lapeled blue suit with a green and blue necktie. He was a tall man at six foot four inches. His short black mustache made him resemble a tall Clark Gable.

"I'm going in early, Al. I think I found something," Rob said.

The couple had worked for the Mestiño Society for seven months, a charity dedicated to preserving the beautiful wild horses of the western United States, and during those seven months, Alison used her marketing skills to increase public donations by a factor of ten. She mailed fliers and pamphlets to horse lovers all over the world. She made hundreds of phone calls to anyone she could find who was interested in horses.

Alison went to Rob for a good morning kiss. She was tall also, five foot ten inches. Her long straight brown hair hung to her shoulders, and her straight and smooth Roman nose was as pretty as her wide eyes.

She had always loved horses, and this was the most satisfying job she ever dreamed of. There were between 75,000 to 140,000 mustangs roaming the west during the 1930's. Now here in 1955 that number has dwindled to 25,000. Helping them survive seemed like a worthy cause.

Alison said, "I'll be in at nine. I need some more sleep. You know I'm sleeping for two now."

"I'll believe that when the doctor says you're sleeping for two."

Rob's position as controller of the charity started to become overwhelming after three months on the job. With Alison bringing in donations, he had to hire two more accountants. In November it looked like they would bring in 12.5 million dollars for that year, 1955.

Rob was never instructed to send any of the money to any organizations that actually helped horses. He was instructed by the board of directors to send the money, in nine-thousand-dollar checks, to a bank in Paris France or a bank in New York City. At first, he assumed that the money was being sent from these banks to the organizations that were dedicated to the wild mustang. This morning he would do some more checking.

When Alison came into the small building in the Mestiño Corral corporate offices, she went to her desk, and got on the phone to try to solicit

VIII. THE ANGEL • 8. In Her Zeros

more charitable donors. At 1:00 p.m. she went to wait for Rob in the lobby. They were going to have a quick lunch.

"Alison, we need to talk."

"Hello Honey. What's going on?" Alison asked.

He guided her to his office and closed the door.

"I've been on the phone all morning. I have called every horse charity there is. I called every animal rescue organization I could find. None of them have ever received any donations from the Mestiño Society. I think this place is a scam."

"Are you sure? I visited the cute little ranch we have in Illinois."

"I'm not sure yet. I need more time. The ranch is on the books, but I think the ranch is there to convince people to give more money. Alison, the board of directors are using your hard work to make millions for themselves. Isn't it funny how we never see the board?"

"That creepy Bob Fournier comes around occasionally. Isn't he on the board?"

"He is."

"Does he look at the books?"

"He does, but I'm not sure he understands them."

Alison said, "So you think Bob Fournier, Clyde Snell, and the brothers Dubois are crooks? That Fournier looks like a crook. I've never seen the others."

⁌⸺⸽⸺⸺⸺⸺

Alison was sitting on the floor in front of the toilet. Her vomiting was long and loud. It had been twelve weeks since she had the premonition that she was pregnant. It was five in the morning.

"Now do you believe me Rob?" Alison said from the bathroom floor in their apartment.

Rob said from their bed, "I think it's just all that Chinese food you ate last night."

"That's another thing, I crave Chinese all the time. Can you get me some?"

"For breakfast?"

"Heat up the leftovers, and I'll love you even more," Allison laughed as she got up from the toilet.

Maggie felt a disruption coming in from all around her, a disruption in the warmth that was her home. The body that surrounded her was not healthy. She could feel the disturbance entering her. It was the worst thing she had ever sensed.

Later that day, Rob McLander found another clue. The Mestiño Society had purchased a restaurant in southern Phoenix called Miss Chili's. He found the books of the business stuffed in an unmarked file cabinet. In 1954 the restaurant showed an incredible revenue of over two million dollars with a profit of twenty-five percent of that. He decided to take Alison there for a Friday evening dinner.

"I wanted Chinese, so why are we here?" Alison asked.

"The Mestiño Society owns this place, Allison," Rob said.

"Really, why would they own a restaurant? It's nice and I like the décor. Doesn't seem to be too busy tonight."

The restaurant was a small Mexican place with about twenty tables. The service and food were just above average. Alison had an enchilada plate while Rob was served Tacos Grande. They both had green margaritas.

"I found the books on it. Can you believe this place is doing over two million? It's only open five days a week."

"That's amazing. The prices are so cheap."

Rob whispered close to Alison, "I think the board is using this place to launder money. I'll bet they have a place in New York and Paris also. Now I know this Mestiño Society is a scam. We work for crooks, and I'm positive they have never helped a horse."

"Well, let's just quit. We can find other jobs."

"Not yet. I have more to do. It might take a couple of months."

In two months, Rob managed to embezzle one and a half million dollars from the charity. He deposited hundreds of small checks into multiple banks around Phoenix. Alison had to work extra hard to keep more money coming into the charity to try to hide the drop-in revenue the embezzlements were causing.

VIII. THE ANGEL • 8. In Her Zeros

"I think you're crazy doing this," Alison said to Rob has they laid in bed before sleep.

"We have to hit them where it hurts: in their wallets. I just need two more weeks and that should do it."

"That creep Fournier was snooping around today. He had a couple of goons with him. They're scary looking." Alison got on her knees and lifted her nighty, "See this bump?"

Alison had a very slight baby bump. Rob put his hand on it.

He said, "It's almost four months now. You need to see a doctor."

"Not while we're in the middle of this. I am going to make sure we are safe. Nobody's going to hurt my baby."

"What are you going to do?"

"You'll find out, and I have a name for our little girl."

"What's that?"

"You'll find that out soon enough also."

⁂

The shop was dark and dusty. The cleanshaven man named Buck was behind the counter. He seemed very knowledgeable. He had on a black cowboy hat.

He spoke to Alison, "This one is exceptionally light weight. It is ideal for a pretty young woman like you."

"I'll take it," Alison said.

Buck said, "Do you want to try it? Do you know how to use it?"

"I'll learn. Do you have one of those for the leg?"

"Yes, I have one that will fit it well."

"I'll take that too."

Alison left the shop feeling a little safer.

⁂

In the corporate office of the Mestiño Society there was a small conference room. There was a big wooden table with eight black office chairs around it. Five men sat around the table. Clyde Snell had called an emergency board meeting.

"I'm glad you all could make it," Clyde said.

He looked like a twenty-six-year-old crime boss. His dark blue suit and thin black necktie made him look older than his years. He tried to be in charge.

"We have a problem," he said.

Sitting around him were three bothers Dubois and Bob Fournier. The French brothers were all short men with black hair and thin black mustaches. They looked like they could be triplets. Only one of them, Louis, could speak English.

Louis said with a thick French accent, "What is problem? Seems everything is going well."

"I have some fairly good proof that our accountant, Rob McLander, is skimming the books. Could be as much as two million," Clyde said.

"Two million!" Fournier said. "Let me kill him."

Clyde said, "In due time. I think he is on to us. Once we get the money back, it will be a bad day for Rob McLander."

Louis Dubois translated the conversation to his brothers Paul and Lucas.

Lucas said in French, *"Good thing I brought this."* He put a black handgun on the conference room table.

"Keep that out," Clyde said. "Bob, bring him in here and bring the wife too. She's in on it."

A few minutes later Bob Fournier returned to the room with Rob and Alison. He had them sit down on two chairs against the wall of the room away from the conference table.

Clyde spoke first, "It's a good morning for us. Not sure it is for you two. You are Rob and Alison?"

Alison said, "Yes, sir, and you are Snell?" She noticed Lucas Dubois pick a gun off the table.

"Yes, now Rob, it seems like you been doing some embezzling. I had another accountant look at the books," Snell said.

Rob responded, "I don't know what you're talking about. The books are in perfect order."

"They are not, and Rob, what have you been doing running around to all these banks the last couple of days? I had you followed."

Alison said, "We know you guys are scamming the donors. We know you haven't helped one horse."

Rob added, "If you let us go we won't go to the authorities and tell them about this so-called operation."

"We can't do that. I want all that money back." Clyde got up from his chair. He walked over to them, pulled his arm back, and punched Alison square in the face as hard as he could.

Blood splattered out of her now-crooked broken nose, covering her long white dress with thick splats of red. Rob tried to get up and go after him. He was stopped when the Frenchman pointed the gun at him.

Snell said, this time with anger, "Again Rob, I want the money back or do you want me to rearrange your wife's face some more?"

Lucas said to his brothers in French, *"This is going to be fun. When we get the money back. I get to shoot them."*

The bleeding Alison watched Lucas closely as he pointed the gun at Rob. When he looked away for a second, she reached into the leg holster under her dress and pulled out her 38 special Smith and Wesson revolver. She fired twice at Lucas hitting him two times in the heart. Lucas grasped his chest and started to fall. The gun fell from his hands, slid across the table, and landed right in front of Rob. Everyone was now standing up. The still bleeding Alison held her gun with two hands and pointed it at Clyde Snell's head.

She said, "If anyone moves, I'll blow his head off. Rob, pick up the gun."

Rob did, and Alison said, "We are going to leave now. If you follow, I will shoot you."

They ran out of the building and got into their 1949 blue Ford. Rob drove the car out of the lot and into the street with the tires screeching.

Alison kept her head turned around to see if they were being followed. Soon a big black 1952 Chrysler came peeling out of the same lot they had just left.

Alison said, "Step on it, Rob, they are following us. Was this worth it Rob? I just killed a man. Now they are chasing us, and we have no money."

Rob shouted, "Where did you get the gun? We do have the money. We have all of it that I stole. I thought they might be on to me, so I removed it from the banks the past couple of days. It's in the trunk of this car."

A gunshot rang out from behind them, shattering the rear window of their car. Alison ducked down below the seat and reloaded her gun. She stuck her head above the seat to see who was after them. "It looks like one of Fournier's goons is driving. Bob is sitting next to him. He has another gun."

Another shot came through the back, skimming the top of the seat, almost hitting Alison. She ducked down below again.

She stuck her upper torso out of the passenger's side window and boldly said, "Nobody's hurting my baby. No one's harming my Maggie!"

Holding her gun with two hands, she fired once at the Chrysler's windshield, shattering it. She fired four more shots towards the bottom of the car, and one of those bullets struck the right front tire. The tire exploded with a bang, forcing the car to turn violently to the right. The vehicle rolled onto its side, then rolled two and a half more times before finally resting with its top on the ground and its wheels up in the air.

As they sped off, Alison could see the goon pulling Bob Fournier out of the smoldering wreak through the passenger's side window.

"Rob, they crashed. Let's go east into New Mexico."

"Why New Mexico?"

"We have to get far away. I don't think they are ever going to stop looking for us."

Rob asked, "Why did you shoot that guy? I could have given them the money back. They might have let us go."

"No, Rob. I speak a little French. That Frenchman said that when they got the money back, he was going to kill us anyway."

Alison moaned, "Oww!"

"Are you okay, Alison? How is your nose?"

"The bleeding stopped, but it's not that. This baby is kicking the shit out of me."

"You called her Maggie? Maybe this is too much excitement for Maggie."

"Maggie is going to live a happy and peaceful life. She will never have to live a day like today. Rob, I have so much love for Maggie."

Rob looked at his wife. "Even with that crooked and broken nose, you still look beautiful."

Maggie felt the pain and stress coming inside her from all around. The body around her was in great distress. Maggie's world seemed to be getting smaller. She was losing the contented feeling she once sensed. Maggie wanted to get out, but at this point, all she could do was kick.

VIII. THE ANGEL • 8. In Her Zeros

Alison was worried about Rob. In the past month they had rented a small apartment in Albuquerque, New Mexico. Rob left a week ago for old Mexico. He wanted to convert some of the cash into some precious metals. Like any accountant, he argued that the cash would lose value over time because of inflation. He knew a dealer in Mexico that could convert the cash, then all Rob had to do was smuggle the precious metals across the border.

Alison was also worried that Rob would get caught bringing illegal gold into the United States. She also had a premonition that Fournier and Snell were getting closer and that they would stop at nothing to get the money back. She also knew that the Dubois brothers would be all focused on avenging the death of their brother Lucas.

It had been over five months since her daughter was conceived. It was getting harder for her to hide her condition. She needed to purchase some supplies and a few books. She would go out tonight, but only under the cover of darkness.

She was relieved when she heard the phone ring. "Hello, Rob?"

He answered back, "Yes, I made it across. I got the gold."

"Okay, get home as soon as possible. I have a feeling Fournier and Snell are getting close. We have to get out of here."

"We can go to the bank tomorrow with a third of the money. Then leave after that. I will be driving all night. Make sure we are packed."

"Rob, you know we are always packed."

The next morning, Alison and Rob turned out of the parking lot of the bank when Allison noticed the man in a car, waiting. She quickly made a right turn, then sped up. She made turn after turn screeching the tires of their Ford with every maneuver.

A startled Rob asked, "What are you doing Alison?"

"I thought I saw one of Fournier's goons in a car at the bank. Is he following us?"

She came to a sign pointing the way to U.S. Highway 85. She got on it northbound pushing the Ford as fast as it would go.

Rob said, "I don't think so, I don't see anybody. Which one was it?"

"It was the ugly one."

"There're both kind of ugly."

Alison replied, "He's the ugly one that's uglier than the ugly one."

Alison had chosen Casper, Wyoming as the place to hide. Hopefully, this would be the last place until the baby arrived. They drove through Colorado going north. By the time they got to the Wyoming border, nightfall had arrived. They would soon rent a place for a few months in the small city and prepare for their new arrival. Most of the houses in Casper had basements.

Rob said to Alison, "Why don't you let me drive, Alison. You've been going for over eight hours."

"No, it keeps my mind off this kicking baby. On the back seat there are a few books. You must study up. You might as well start now."

Rob reached back and took the books. They were titled *Midwives, a Modern Instruction*, *The Successful Midwife*, the last was, *Birthing Methods of the Midwife*.

Rob said, "These are about Midwives. Are we going to use one?"

"No Rob, you're going to do it."

"Alison, I can't. I'm an accountant, I can't do this. What if something goes wrong?"

"Nothing will go wrong. You will study this so you can't make a mistake," Alison said quickly.

"We need to take you to a hospital. This is your first birth and there could be an emergency."

"We can't. I know you are an accountant, but your accounting got us into this mess. No one can know that Maggie exists. If these creeps that are chasing us find out, they will kill her along with us."

"This is too crazy," Rob said in a panic. "I'm willing to turn myself into the police. That way you and Maggie can have a safe birth."

"No way, my husband. They would get me as an accessory. Rob, did you forget already? I shot a guy."

They found a small red wooden house, fully furnished, for rent in a lower middle-class neighborhood in Casper. It had two bedrooms and two baths and one of the baths had a large old-fashioned oval bathtub. The basement was unfinished.

Alison was now in her seventh month of pregnancy. She had not left the house since they moved. She was extremely uncomfortable and ready to get preparations for the baby started. Alison got up from bed one Saturday morning and started giving Rob orders.

"I need you to pick up some things today. Don't forget to take the gun," she told him.

"What do you need?"

"It's time to get ready. We need blankets, towels, diapers, thermometers, garbage bags, a flashlight, just to name a few. Let's go through the books and make a list. I also need you to go to the hardware store and pick up everything you need to get that big tub into the basement."

"Why do we need that down there?" Rob asked.

"I want to do a water birth. I don't want the neighbors to hear my screams or a baby cry."

"It's a free-standing tub. All I need to do is disconnect the drain and faucets. It won't be easy getting it down there. That thing weighs a ton."

"I'll help," Alison said.

"You're not in any condition to help lift that thing."

"I said I'll help, and I will."

Maggie needed to get out. The kicking was doing no good. She felt pain and discomfort. There wasn't enough room, and the body around her was sending her messages of stress and irritation. She sensed this body was worse off than she was. The déjà vu she sensed was telling her it was time. It also told her she was not in the right position. She was upside-down.

At 11:00 p.m. on a Saturday, Alison got up from her bed.

She announced to Rob, "It's time. Let's go to the basement."

They had a twin bed and a small basinet set up near the bathtub. There was a small table nearby with all the birthing supplies organized neatly on top. Rob started filling a bucket with warm water from a basement sink and transferring it to the tub.

Alison was in her bathrobe, "Don't get it too hot Rob."

Rob put a thermometer into the bucket, "It's right at ninety-two degrees."

"That will work. I think I have been in labor for over eight hours. Maggie should come sometime early Sunday morning."

Alison lay on the bed for two more hours. When she felt the urge to push, she got up and took off her bathrobe. Rob helped the naked woman get into the tub.

Rob said, "I know the answer, but are you sure the baby won't drown?"

"Yes, the baby is in water now. We are just transferring her to different water. Rob, it hurts so bad. It feels like my insides are being twisted into a spiral. I'm going to push."

"Push gently, Alison."

She started screaming louder and louder until she finally yelled, "Get out of me girl!"

Rob tried to stay calm. "I see her starting to come out."

"Do you see the head?" Alison yelled.

"No, I see the feet and legs."

"Oh my god! She is breech. That is the wrong way. It's killing me, I think you were right Rob, we should have gone to the hospital."

Rob told her, "No, I got this. Just keep pushing gently."

When the baby's legs were fully exposed, Rob took a small towel and folded it lengthwise. He put the towel in the water and wrapped it around the baby's legs.

He said, "Keep pushing. She is halfway out, and Alison, she is a girl."

Alisson cried, "I know that you bastard! How much longer?"

"A little more. I see the bottom of her face."

Alison pushed some more, and the baby was released into the warm water. Rob put one hand under Maggie's back and the other under her head. He gently lifted her out of the water and handed her to Alison. Rob cut the umbilical cord.

"Give me a towel." Alison demanded.

"Is she all right? Shouldn't she be crying?" Rob asked.

"I don't think that's required. She is breathing fine. She just opened her eyes. She is so perfect."

Rob went behind Alison so he could see. "She is perfect. She has a lot of light brown hair."

"I'm going to put a yellow bow in it."

VIII. THE ANGEL • 8. In Her Zeros

The couple spent the next half hour admiring Maggie. Then the exhausted Alison said to Rob, "Take her and put her in the basinet. I'm going to get out now."

Rob put the baby in the basinet, then helped his wife out of the tub. He dried her off and helped her get into a long white nightgown. She got into the small bed by the basinet.

"You have to clean this up Rob. This time I can't help you."

"I will do it now."

Rob cleaned up the mess, then got into a sleeping bag next to Alison's bed. Two of the three were soon fast asleep. One of them was not.

⁂

Maggie could see for the first time. She saw patches of light and patches of dark. Soon, the lighted patches turned into colors. She saw yellows, reds, and blues for the first time. She did not want to sleep. She did not want to cry. She did want to learn about this world for the first time. She saw the image of a Being above her. This was not the body that gave her life. Inspector Lawrence was kneeling next to the bassinet looking at her.

"Hello Maggie, this is the first time in a while that I have enjoyed being an angel," he said. "I think your parents are going to sleep for a while. Since you are so young, I decided not to smoke."

Maggie looked back at the man. She made a few gurgling noises and moved her little hands and feet rapidly in the air.

The Inspector continued, "I don't think you can understand me. But knowing you, I wouldn't be surprised if you could."

Maggie was still staring at the Being.

"You amaze me every time I examine you. Here you are, only a few hours old and your eyes are already a vibrant green. That's not supposed to happen for months."

Maggie looked at the man. She understood perfectly everything he was saying.

"I'm going to do this as gently as I can."

The Inspector softly touched Maggie's forehead.

Maggie's mind exploded.

⁂

IX. THE ANGEL

The five Beings that make up the Consul are kind of like the leadership group of a large company existing on the Below World. They run the daily operations of everything going on in the Bliss. They make difficult decisions and make sure all Beings are happy and content. They constantly review Company Bliss to ensure the procedures are efficient and honest.

The Consul runs things, but they don't own the show. The creator of all we know is one we call The Master. We use the pronoun one because we do not know if The Master is a female Being or a male Being—or both. Only the members of the Consul have been in The Master's presence. They might be there right now. I have heard rumors that the Consul will go to The Master for advice on their toughest decisions. Maybe they are being wishy-washy with their decision on what to do with Maggie; maybe they need The Master's advice.

The big shots upstairs do have a lot of responsibilities, but us Inspectors are the ones down in the field doing the dirty work. It's a relief that they are gone for a while because it gives me time to conduct another examination. There must have been a reason Maggie was escaping to France after my first exam. I don't think this was a vacation.

Why was Paris the destination of Maggie Love?

9. In Her Fifties

MAGGIE WOKE UP.

She was in a bright spinning room and the sound of the rapidly revolving, rotating, and turning made her feel like she was in the middle of a tornado. She couldn't hear through the howling wind, and she couldn't see through the blurry madness. She could smell, and her keen sense picked up the scent of fresh blood. When the spinning began to settle, she saw she was behind a fully stretched-out black leather recliner chair. There was a TV on in front of the chair, showing a news program in the French language. The howling wind started to quiet down, and she finally could hear. No doubt that this was the sound of a man gasping for air. Very soon the wheezing noise stopped. The seventy-something grey-haired man in the chair had blood pouring out of his sliced throat. Maggie had a hunting knife in her right hand.

"Where am I? What did I do?" Maggie whispered to herself.

Memories started to come back to her. "This is the brother, Paul Dubois. My mom killed Lucas. Now there is only one more left." Maggie fought with her memory. "There is something else I'm supposed to do. Oh yes, now I remember"

Maggie took a letter-sized envelope out of her back pocket. She made sure she got some blood smeared on the front. Printed on the sealed envelope in capital letters was the name DUBOIS. She stuffed it into the dead man's pants front pocket.

Maggie got out of the small house in suburban Paris quickly. It was nighttime. She went out the back and easily scaled a two-meter wooden fence. In the alley behind the house was a black Volkswagen bug waiting for her. She got in, reached under the seat to find her small yellow handbag. She found a passport inside. She turned on the light and adjusted the rear-view mirror of the car to see her face. She thought she looked pretty for a fifty-three-year-old. Her hair was deep red. It was shoulder length and wavy, with big curls on the ends. The picture on the passport matched the reflection in the mirror. The name on the passport read Tommie Scott. She looked at the iPhone she had in her pocket. The year was 2009. Maggie knew exactly where she was.

◦∞◦

Louis Dubois arrived at his brother's house along with his two sons and rang the doorbell. Paul Dubois' son, Richard, opened the door for his uncle and two cousins.

Richard spoke in French, "*Somebody killed my father. They cut his throat open.*"

Richard was a tall man. He was heavy but not fat. Most would call him stocky. He had black hair and the short Dubois mustache.

He went on, "*They left the knife in a pool of blood on the chair where they killed him.*"

"*We know that Richard. Somebody killed my only surviving brother. Now I am the only brother left. Show us the crime scene,*" Louis Dubois said.

Louis Dubois had just celebrated his eightieth birthday. The six-footer was gray and mostly bald but looked in fairly good shape for a man of his years. He had to be. He was in charge—the the family patriarch.

The four men walked into a small den in the rear of the house. There the bloody corpse laid in the chair, just as Maggie had left it.

"*I haven't touched anything. This is just as I found him,*" Richard said.

His cousin Frédéric said, "*That's good Richard. We do not want to contaminate the crime scene. Did you call the police? Look at him. He's lying in a pool of his own blood.*"

Frédéric was the only Dubois that refused to wear the Dubois mustache. He was much smaller than his brother Alexander. Frédéric had the skinny nerd look going on with his thick rimmed glasses and crew-cut brown hair.

His father interrupted, "*No, police! This is a Dubois matter. We will handle it our way.*"

Frédéric said in a nerdy scared voice, "*I disagree father. This is a serious crime. We should go to the authorities.*"

IX. THE ANGEL • 9. In Her Fifties

Frédéric's brother, Alexander, didn't resemble his thin brother at all. He was tall and stocky and looked much more like his cousin Richard. He barked at his brother in loud French, *"Listen to Father. We do what he says. Act like a Dubois not a coward, Frédéric!"*

"Thank you, Alexander," the old patriarch said. *"We will treat this like it was a suicide. My dear brother's Alzheimer's disease was getting worse. He took his own life, and we have no time to morn now. We must find out who did this and handle it our way. With as much pain and suffering as we can give to this criminal. Check the body for clues."*

Alexander stood above his dead uncle. He patted down his blood splattered body then checked his khaki pants. Stuffed in one of the pockets was a bloody envelope with the name DUBOIS printed on the front. He handed it to his father, Louis.

The patriarch opened it and tried to read the note inside. *"It's in English. I speak it some, but I cannot read it. Frédéric, I let you go to that fancy college in the US."*

"Yes father. Yale university. I majored in English."

Louis handed Frédéric the note. *"Read it to us."*

Frédéric looked at the note. *"It seems to be some sort of riddle."* He read it out loud in perfect English, "Who am I that committed this crime? I may be Molly. Never ask why. Drop the why. Gee, join the Army and add everything. E is for everything. I can never feel love. It is impossible for me to feel love, because I am Love. You need to learn Spanish."

"Read it in French, Frédéric," Louis firmly said.

Frédéric said back, *"I can translate it into French, but I think to solve the riddle, it has to be done in English."*

"Okay, just solve it. How long will it take?"

"Give me a day or two."

"Finally, I'm going to get some payback on that fortune I spent to get you through college,"

Louis started giving orders. *"Richard, get some of the boys over here. Have them make this look as much like a suicide as possible. Alexander, as soon as that is done, call the cops and the morgue. Get the body out of here. Frédéric, solve that riddle. One day is better than two. Let us all meet at the nonprofit tomorrow at 17:00. We can discuss our next steps."*

Louis knew they had many enemies, many that wanted them dead. But he felt that this had something to do with what happened years ago, about fifty-four years ago to be exact, the day his brother Lucas was shot by Alison McLander.

Maggie sat comfortably in her first-class seat. She had three flights to get through, Paris to New York, New York to Los Angeles, and finally, L.A. to Cabo San Lucas, Mexico. She needed a few days to prepare for some visitors. She did not need too much time. She had been preparing for this for over a year. The visitors from Paris would be welcomed with open arms.

Nonprofits worked out well for the Dubois clan. This one in Paris, *The Homeless Hound*, was doing fine. They did manage to give two cents on the euro to help homeless animals. They spent ten cents a euro on operations and marketing. The rest went to the clan. The Dubois family was prosperous. They needed to find out who was trying to change their world.

The four Dubois men sat in a small conference room at *The Homeless Hound* headquarters to discuss what to do about the murder of Paul Dubois.

Frédéric seemed unusually excited and nervous. "*I solved the riddle and much more,*" he told the group. "*Before I go on, Father, I researched the American partners you had in a nonprofit years ago.*"

"Yes, one died a couple of years ago. The other at least twenty years ago. I think they were both deemed accidents," Louis answered.

"I'm positive they were not accidents. The person that killed Uncle Paul killed those two men also. The partners names were Robert 'Bob' Fournier and Clyde Snell."

Alexander said to his brother, "Frédéric, calm down. You sound scared. Your voice is all shaky. Now tell us about the riddle."

"The riddle reveals her name, and it is not Molly. Molly is one of her aliases. I would bet she has hundreds of those. Her name in English is Maggie Love, and I have more, much more."

"Go on, Frédéric," the elder Louis said.

"I checked into the deaths of Fournier and Snell. Father told me Fournier changed his name to Baker and became a United States Congressmen. They

IX. THE ANGEL • 9. In Her Fifties

found the Congressman hanging dead in a rented house in Washington DC. He was in a most unflattering position. A week before he died, he hired an assistant named Molly Jones. The cops tried to find her. They could not and she seemed to have just vanished. That is the Molly in the riddle."

His cousin Richard said, *"So, this Maggie Love killed my father, Fournier, and Snell?"*

"Just a couple of years ago, they found Snell in the bottom of a subway track in New York. A train ran him over and tore him into hundreds of pieces. Snell had just married a woman named Anita Hamilton. Six months later he was dead. Hamilton was never found. That is because Hamilton is another alias of Maggie Love."

Richard questioned him, *"I don't believe one woman could do all this. I need more proof."*

Frédéric opened his laptop computer. He connected it to a big screen TV in the conference room. *"I have proof, and I don't believe she's a woman. At least not a human woman. Here is the proof. The riddle says we need to learn Spanish. I spent hours checking records in Spain. I found nothing. I tried Mexico next and after hours and hours of searching the net, I found a restaurant leased by a Sally Love. It was called Sara's Mexican Heat. They have a web site."*

Suddenly, a picture of a beautiful restaurant with a canopy stretching over a sandy beach appeared on the big screen.

Frédéric continued, *"This site has eight pages. I studied it for hours and hours. I found it on the bar page."*

The page changed to show a long bar with colorful bottles of liquor shining behind it. There were two bartenders working with six customers sitting on stools in front of the bar.

Frédéric started shaking even worse. *"See this woman standing behind the bar staring at the camera? She has a Mona Lisa-type smile."*

Frédéric zoomed in on the picture of the woman on the right side of the bar.

Louis commented, *"A very attractive woman. Looks like she's in her early thirties."*

"Father, I think she is in her middle fifties, and Father, this is Maggie Love."

Alexander asked, *"How can you be so sure?"*

Frédéric zoomed in on the name tag pinned above her left breast. It read "Hola, My Name is Anita Hamilton."

"That can't be a coincidence, and there is more."

On the bar in front of her was something that looked like a long desk nameplate. Frédéric zoomed in on the it. There were three groups of six letters. They were all capital. They were ICFICS MMACLD IMGTCU.

Richard asked, *"What is that? Are they Spanish words?"*

Frédéric replied, *"No. It is English. I studied this for hours and hours, and I finally realized in English the C and the K can make the same sound. When I replaced Cs with Ks, I had it."*

"What does it mean?" Alexander asked.

Frédéric's voice stared to crack. *"I'm going to say this in English. I think you will all understand.* Here is the first one. IKFIKS means 'I killed Fournier. I killed Snell'."

"No way," Richard said loudly.

"The second one, MMAKLD means, 'My Ma killed Lucas Dubois'."

Louis stood up. "Wait a minute, Alison McLander killed my brother. The McLanders did not have any children."

"I believe they did Father. They had one."

Louis said, "The people we had searching for them found the dead bodies of the McLanders in a basement. They said there were toys, a bed, and a doll house down there."

Frédéric continued, "Here is the third, IMGTKU. *This one is scaring me to death.* It means, 'I am going to kill you'." The trembling Frédéric switched back to French, *"I only slept an hour last night. When I finally fell asleep, I had a nightmare. Maggie Love was standing over my bed with a knife."*

Alexander yelled at his brother, *"Frédéric, calm down and act like a Dubois. We can easily handle one woman."*

Frédéric was starting to whimper, *"This is not a woman."*

Frédéric zoomed in on the eyes of the woman on the big screen. "Look at those eyes. No human has eyes that vibrant green. She doesn't seem to age at all. Father thought she was thirty, and she is around fifty-three. She changes identities any time she wants. It is almost like she alters her form. Next time you pick up a baguette at a bakery, Maggie Love might be behind the counter, and you would never know it."

"This is what I'm going to do," Cousin Richard said. "I'm going to go to Mexico and kill that murdering bitch."

Frédéric was quick to reply, "Richard, don't do that. That is exactly what she wants us to do. You will be playing ball on her home turf. You all do not understand. This woman is some kind of a wizard."

Frédéric stood up. He started speaking English in a crying screech, "She's not a wizard. She's not a wiz… Maggie Love is a witch! I'm getting the hell out of here."

He grabbed his computer and ran out of the conference room.

Louis stayed calm. He said to his son, "*Alexander, go get him and bring him back here.*"

When Alexander returned with Frédéric, the smaller son said, "*Father, I'm sorry. I got so upset when I saw Uncle Paul murdered like that. One other thing I did not get to say. I believe she has a son and boyfriend in Mexico.*"

"Sit down," Louis stood up and started walking slowly around the table. "*This is what we are going to do. Richard, I like your idea about going to Mexico. You and Alexander take a couple of the boys and go have a little vacation. I never told you this, but the McLanders got away with a lot of our money. I am sure this Maggie Love has it.*"

"*How much?*" Richard asked.

"*Fifty years ago, it was over two million dollars. Here is what you do. You find this son and boyfriend and take them hostage. When this Maggie contacts you, tell her you want a ransom of twelve million.*"

"*Yes father, inflation and interest,*" Frédéric said.

"*When you get the money, kill all three of them. I hear they have kidnappings and hostage-takings all the time in Mexico. Should be a piece of cake. Frédéric. Where in Mexico is this Maggie Love?*"

"*In southern Baja, California. A resort town called Cabo San Lucas.*"

Louis laughed and said, "*My brother is the saint to all of this family. It is ironic how the woman whose mother killed my brother Lucas is going to die in The Cape of Saint Lucas.*"

⁕

It was 6:00 a.m. in the morning when the doorbell rang. James Cannon was in the shower.

"Bruce, get the door. I'm in the shower!" he yelled.

Bruce Love-Cannon slowly crawled out of bed and stood up. The twenty-year-old had grown to be two inches taller than his mother and father. He had his father's curly hair and light amber skin. He did not inherit his mother's green eyes. His were light brown like his father's. He slowly made his way out of his bed and towards the front door of the villa. He opened it.

With a surprised look on his face he said, "Mom? You're back?"

Maggie gave Bruce a slight kiss on the cheek. "Of course, I'm back. I may stay awhile this time."

"It's been over a year. Don't I get a hug?" Bruce asked.

"I'm not a hugging person, you know that. So, where's your father?"

"He's in the shower. You know he wasn't too happy with you when you left the last time."

"I'm not here to make him happy."

"Mom, where do you go all these times?"

"Brucie," Maggie had a carry-on suitcase and a meter-tall bright orange canister outside the door. "Those canisters are too heavy for your mom. I have five more in the back of a small red truck out front. Will my big boy help his mom and bring them in?"

"What are they?"

"Just some fire extinguishers."

Bruce asked, "Why do we need six fire extinguishers?"

Maggie smiled and said, "You can never be too careful nowadays."

She took her suitcase and rolled it towards the bedroom. Maggie opened the door and entered. A nude James was drying off in the master bath. He saw Maggie and quickly put on his bath robe.

He said with a little disdain, "You're back? Don't you know how to knock?"

"Hello James. You look good and lost a little weight I see. Why should I knock? This is my house."

"Maggie, I know you're not going to tell me, but where did you go? You were gone for another year or so. I just can't take the pain anymore."

"Yes, you can." Maggie took off his bathrobe and put her arms around him. James would be very late for his work at the hotel.

∼

Bruce brought in all the extinguishers and put them in the center of the living room along with a few boxes Maggie had him bring into the villa.

James was rushing out the door when he saw them. "What are these canisters for, Maggie?"

"Just some fire extinguishers."

James asked, "Why do we need six fire extinguishers?"

"You can't be too careful, nowadays. Bruce, put the four orange ones in the corners of this room. The two red ones go on each side of the bed in our bedroom," Maggie ordered.

"Why don't they say anything on them? They are just colorful big cylinders."

Maggie answered, "I painted them. If we are going to have them in our house, they should go with the décor. Bruce gets off tonight at eight. When he does, I want the three of us to play a game."

"I've known you a long time. I never remember you playing games before," James said.

"I'm trying to be a new Maggie Love. By playing games, I can get to know my two big men much better."

꧁꧂

"I win!" Maggie gloated. "Now we get Chinese food all week long."

"No Mom. I hate Chinese," Bruce protested.

James added, "I don't think this is much of a game, a holding-your-breath contest?"

"It's good for your stamina. You would think two big strong men could beat a girl, but it wasn't even close. I held mine for two and a half minutes Bruce for fifty seconds, and James was dead last at forty-five seconds. That was so funny, Bruce. Your father was turning purple."

"I want another chance," Bruce said. "I can't take a whole week of Chinese food."

Maggie replied, "You two keep practicing. I will give you another chance tomorrow. I wanted to show you two these things I bought." Maggie pulled out a black mask with two large eyeholes covered by plastic with a large beige disk-type filter over the nose.

"Gas masks? What do we need those for?" James asked.

"James, do you know that more deaths in fires are caused by smoke inhalation than the actual fire itself? I have three of these. I am placing them behind the furniture. Remember where they are in case we have a fire."

"Why are you so worried about fires all of the sudden?" James inquired.

"You know how eccentric I am. If you want to be the boyfriend of Maggie Love, you must learn to live with it. There's one more thing, James and Bruce."

"What now?" James asked with concern.

"The drug trade around here is out of control. The neighborhood is going to shit. I have some guys coming tomorrow to upgrade the windows. I'm also having them put security bars on all of them."

"Bars? We live in a gated community," James said, trying hard not to show any emotion.

"One more thing. I'm upgrading all the door locks, inside and out. You just can't be too careful nowadays. Try to hold your breath for two minutes. If you can make it to two and a half, I won't get my Chinese food."

⁓⁓⁓

After a week of prep, Maggie knew the time was coming soon. Everything was ready. James and Bruce could now hold their breath for almost two minutes. Maggie still got her Chinese food for the week.

The bizarre escapade started on a Sunday morning. James was on the street side of the Hotel Excelsior where his short break would soon be interrupted. A blue Ford SUV quickly pulled up beside him. Two blond goons got out and surrounded him. One of them had a handgun who poked it into James's gut. Then they forced him to sit in the back seat in-between them.

"What do you guys what?" James said in Spanish.

Alexander and Richard Dubois were sitting in the front seat. Alexander was driving.

Richard turned around to look at James. He was holding a handgun over the seat.

He spoke English with a thick French accent, "We have been watching you, James. Let's go to your house and visit your son. Now, where is this Maggie Love? She owes us a lot of money."

"I don't know any Maggie Love."

Richard continued, "Come on man, don't play with us. She will come. You will call her when we get to your house. If she does not come you and your son will have a very short life."

James Cannon unlocked the door of the villa. The two blond goons pushed him inside. The five men were soon greeted by Bruce.

IX. THE ANGEL • 9. In Her Fifties

He said, "Dad, who are these guys?"

"I don't know, Bruce. They want to talk to your mom," James said with a shaky voice.

Richard and the gun-toting goon pointed their weapons at them.

Alexander gave the orders, "You two sit on this couch. James, you call this Maggie Love now."

James took his cell phone and rang her. He heard three beeps then she picked up. "Hello James. What's up?" Maggie said from some unknown location.

James answered, "There are four men here at home. They want to see you. I think they mean right away."

Maggie calmly replied, "Oh good. They are here. I've been expecting them. I love the French people."

"What?" James said.

"Just stay calm, James. I will be there shortly. I need to talk to one of them."

James handed the phone to Alexander Dubois. He said into James's phone, "Is this Maggie Love?"

Maggie spoke in French, *"Yes, it is. I'll give you what you want, just don't hurt them."*

Alexander replied, *"Yes, we won't hurt them. What we want is twelve million American dollars. When we get it, everyone will be fine. We know you killed a congressman, a businessman, and my uncle Paul."*

Maggie said, *"I have two million in untraceable Mexican gold. I can give you that right now. The rest will come tomorrow."*

"I want it all now Madam or these two die."

"It's Sunday. The banks are closed. Let me bring you the gold, and we can talk about the rest."

"Okay Maggie Love. You had better hurry. You don't want an accident."

"I will be there shortly. Just don't hurt them."

☙

Maggie opened the door to the villa. She closed the door, making sure it was securely latched. Maggie handed a large briefcase to one of the goons.

She calmly said in English, "It is nice to meet you all. I am Maggie Love. I love the French people so much."

Richard said in French, "*So you are the murderer that killed my father. You don't look like a witch. You look more like a bitch.*"

Alexander ordered the goons, "*Frisk her. Check her legs. When her mother killed my uncle Lucas, she hid the gun in a leg holster.*"

Maggie didn't have a gun. What she had strapped to her right thigh was a remote control, one that she had previously connected to each of the six canisters. The aggressive frisking by the blond goon set Maggie's plan into motion.

Maggie heard it trip. She looked at James and Bruce and loudly said, "Two minutes in five, four, three, two, now!"

A loud hissing noise erupted from each of the orange canisters. They were spraying the room with a colorless and odorless gas. The high concentration of hydrogen cyanide gas made the four Frenchmen immediately start to cough and choke. As the room filled with poison, they started to panic. James and Bruce knew exactly what to do.

The coughing Richard yelled in French, "*Go outside!*"

The frisking blond goon tried to open the door. There was a numeral keypad above the knob, "*It's locked,*" he said. "*You need some kind of combination.*"

"*Shoot it out!*" Richard ordered.

He fired four shots at the doorknob, accomplishing nothing.

Richard ordered again, "*Shoot out the window!*"

The blond moved the curtains away from a window near the door. He fired twice at the window. The bullets lodged in the glass, but the thick material refused to break.

"*It's no good. There are bars there anyway.*" The goon's coughing got more violent. He went down on all fours.

Richard pointed his gun at Bruce. He said to Maggie, "*You stop this, or I will kill your boy.*"

He saw they were both wearing gas masks. He erupted into more violent coughs, and James saw an opening. With both goons shaking and convoluting on the floor, James jumped at Richard and tackled him. The gun flew out of Richard's hand and landed next to the crouching and vomiting Alexander.

Alexander took the gun. He yelled his last words, "*Frédéric was right. Maggie Love is a witch!*"

He fired four times, each shot hitting Maggie in the chest. The force of the bullets threw her back until she landed flat on her back. As the four Frenchmen died, James and Bruce rushed to her side. Bruce put the third gas mask over Maggie's face.

She pushed it away and tried not to breathe in. "Take me into our bedroom."

James said through the mask, "Maggie, there are canisters in there also."

Maggie shot back, "Yes James, but those are filled with oxygen."

James picked Maggie up and carried her to the bedroom. Maggie had put the keypad locks on all the doors in the villa. Bruce was ahead of them. He punched in the combination 4-4-4-8. The bedroom door opened. James gently put Maggie on the bed. Her shirt was stained in the middle of her chest with a growing spot of blood.

Maggie kept repeating, "I will not go into shock. I will not go into shock. James, open my blouse. I will not go into shock."

James said to Bruce, "Bruce, call an ambulance. Your mom has been hit."

Maggie struggled to say, "Bruce, don't you dare! I'm not going into shock. I'm not going into shock."

James ripped the buttons off her blouse. "Maggie, you're wearing a bullet-proof vest."

"I guess I didn't plan this well enough, I should have worn two. One bullet got through." Maggie voice was getting softer. "I'm not going into shock. I don't think the bullet entered my heart. James, keep putting pressure on it. Try to stop the bleeding. James, I have three antidote kits for the poison under the bed. All three of us will have to go through the procedure."

James took off his mask and kissed her cheek. He got close to her ear. "Maggie, we have to get you to a doctor."

"No doctors for Maggie Love. Bruce, keep your mask on. Go into the kitchen. Take knives tweezers, scissors, and anything else we might need and boil them. I have some vodka in the top drawer in the kitchen. Bring it."

"What about those guys out there?" Bruce asked.

Maggie tried to laugh through the pain. "Bruce, they're all dead by now. James you are going to get this bullet out of me."

"I can't Maggie. I'm no doctor."

"You can. I will coach you through it. I will not go into shock. I will not go into shock. James, am I a witch like the Frenchman said?"

Maggie started to black out. She knew that she had to use the power of her mind to stay awake and not go into shock. When things started to clear up, the man looking at her from above was not James.

"No, no, Inspector no. Not now. I am dying. I have to coach James on how to do this."

The Inspector whispered to her, "No Maggie. You don't have to go through this again. I have seen enough."

He moved his hand toward her forehead.

Maggie said, "Wait Inspector. Answer me one question before you do this."

"Okay Maggie. What do you want to ask?"

"Am I a witch like the Frenchman said? I bring death everywhere I go. Am I a witch?"

The Inspector answered, "No, Maggie. You are not a witch. I'll tell you what you are. You are totally brilliant."

Maggie's mind exploded.

X. THE ANGEL

I once told you that Maggie Love had no moral code. I implied that she killed indiscriminately with a twinkle in her eye and a smile on her face. For the most part, I was wrong. The more exams I preform, the more I know I was wrong. Maggie does have a moral code, so let me call it Maggie's Code. She does things on her timeline in her own unique way. Maggie's Code is to look at a problem, think it through, then solve it in one big swoosh. If murder is the solution, then murder she will.

I still can't tell if Maggie really cares for her family or are they just there for some occasional amusement. She comes and goes as she pleases, and it seems like she was never there to raise her only son. James seems to be a marvelous fellow. In fact, it seems like James is more of a family member than Maggie ever was.

I have not heard anything from the Consul in a while. As far as I can tell, no decision on Maggie Love has been made. Another exam will surely happen, and I'm going to be called on to go in again. I hope we finish this soon. I don't know how much more I can take.

※

Sure enough, I have to do this again. You know, I did see that Maggie does have a sense of humor, especially when she was younger. Let me see if I can go back earlier and find a more sociable, even happier Maggie Love.

10. In Her Twenties

MAGGIE WOKE UP.

She felt enclosed, like she was in a cage. The spinning and whirling were quite violent, and she sensed there were four barriers around her. She was sitting down, and her short red pants were down to her knees. As the dizziness increased, she wanted to throw up and she felt this was the perfect place to do that.

As the whirling started to subside, she heard a voice from outside her barrier. The voice was female, and it had a very tangy southern accent.

"Girl, are you okay? You've been in there forever. You didn't fall in, did ya? I'm goin' back out there. I wanna dance."

Maggie stood up and pulled up her shorts. She flushed the toilet and opened the stall door. She noticed that she had her small yellow handbag flung over her shoulders. Maggie went to one of four sinks to wash her hands. She took a long look at the reflection in the mirror above the basin. She did not recognize the face staring back at her.

In her handbag she found a driver's license. The name on it read Molly Jones. The ID picture did not match the reflection in the mirror. She noticed another license behind that one and this one certainly did match.

She did a double-take and looked in the mirror again. She saw a young woman with blond hair molded into two braided pigtails, each one hanging two inches below her breasts. Her eyes were a bright blue and she saw that she had what looked like light brown freckles scattered across her face. The red and yellow flowered backless blouse she wore went perfectly with her red shorts. There was a white cowboy hat with a thick black band on the counter next to the sink.

"That's mine," she said to herself with a thick, happy southern accent.

She put on the hat and adjusted it, so it was tipped upwards. The woman wanted to see her full face.

Maggie didn't know why she blurted this out, but she blurted it out anyway, "Man girl! You one good lookin' babe. You one fine lookin' girl, Bonnie Dickerson!"

―――

Maggie left the restroom to find a crowded county and western bar. A juke box by a large dance floor was blaring out Conway Twitty's country song "Tight Fittin' Jeans." The lights in Little Miss Whisky's establishment were mostly colored a florescent purple. Maggie had no idea why she was here. Memories started to come back inside her brain, and she remembered that she was here with a friend, and her name was…Cindy Taylor. That was it. Maggie recognized her sitting by herself at the bar in the back.

Maggie sat next to her as she said to the bartender, "I'll have a Coke please."

Cindy said to her, "You were in there long enough. I was ready to organize a search party to try to find you."

"I'm so sorry, kid. I just got so dizzy. I almost threw up."

Cindy said in her tangy southern drawl, "How could you be barfin'? You haven't even had one drink. You don't have a bun in the oven, do ya girl?"

Cindy had a masculine but pretty face. Her hair was long, straight, and jet black. She was a tall woman but still an inch shorter than Maggie.

Maggie replied, "No momma. I ain't got no bun in the oven. I just got a little sick."

The bartender placed a Coke down in front of Maggie.

"Bonnie, that's what's makin' you sick. It's all that damn Coke you drink. Why don't you put some booze in there?" Cindy asked.

"I ain't drinkin' that stuff. I don't like it."

"I know what you are Bonnie. You're just a goody two-shoes."

"I'm not no goody two-shoes. I done lots of bad stuff." Maggie made her southern accent sound just like Cindy's North Carolina drawl.

Cindy said, "Unless you killed someone that I don't know about, I'd say you're a double damn goody two-shoes."

"Shut up Cindy. Let's go out there and dance."

Cindy noticed someone across the large dance floor.

X. THE ANGEL • 10. In Her Twenties

"Damn it," Cindy said. "My boss is here. I told him I'd be here, and it looks like we might have to cut this date short."

"Is he your boss or your pimp?"

"Same difference."

"Cindy, you got to quit that shit," Maggie said.

"I told you. I'm just doing this for one more year. Then I'll have enough money to go back to college. I'll be Cindy Taylor, a professional attorney. That's a fancy way to say lawyer."

"That sounds better than Cindy Tayler, professional female escort."

A large man made his way across the dance floor toward the bar. He stopped and said to Cindy, "Sorry young lady. I got you a client tonight. He paid in full and expects you at the hotel in an hour."

Jake Boras was a short and hefty man. His full two-inch-long black beard looked dirty and even in the dim light of the country bar, he wore dark glasses. He was dressed in a biker's leather jacket with torn denim jeans.

"I gotta go, Bonnie. This was fun while it lasted," Cindy said.

Jake looked at Maggie, "Who is this lovely specimen of a woman?"

Cindy said, "Jake, Bonnie. Bonnie, Jake."

Maggie got up to shake his hand.

Jake took off the dark glasses and checked her out. "Wow wee. You are a tall one, taller than me. If you ever need some quick money, I will have no problem getting you the best and highest paying clients."

Maggie answered, "No thanks, I got a good job at the Walmart."

"Walmart?" Jake acted surprised. "I fine specimen like you should not be working at the Walmart."

Cindy said to Bonnie as she walked away, "Maybe we can get together next week."

Maggie quickly asked, "Before you go, can you tell me what year this is?"

Cindy said with her thickest southern drawl, "Come on girl, maybe that bartender did put some booze in your coke. It is 1981."

Maggie finished her Coke then got out of the place. In the parking lot she noticed a red Volkswagen bug and she immediately remembered that it was hers. She got in the car and started it up with a key she had in her yellow handbag. She didn't know where she was going. That memory was not in her head yet.

"Of course," she said to herself. "I have an apartment on 12th Street here in DC. It's only about four miles away."

She made the short drive, parked her car in the lot, and went into the light brown building. She walked in through the main entrance and found an elevator near the lobby. She pushed the button three. Maggie got out of the elevator and walked down the hall until she found a door with a 321 placed on it. She opened the door with another key she had in her bag.

It was a small one-room studio with a full bath and a small kitchenette. Maggie could afford better. She knew she had plenty of money. The hotel and restaurant in Mexico were doing quite well.

Maggie remembered she had been living in Washington DC for over four years now, with only an occasional visit to Mexico. She had not found any specific hints about her past. She knew they were here, here in DC. It was not the time yet to go back to her Mexican home. She thought about planning another visit to see her foster mom, Sally, soon.

She looked in her closet and saw all the drab-colored and boring business suits. She would spend one more day as Bonnie Dickerson. That was much more fun, but come Monday, she would go back to her job at a law firm as the lackluster secretary, Molly Jones.

Maggie was getting ready for bed when her phone rang.

She picked it up and said in a very non-distinct voice, "Hello."

"Is this you, Bonnie? This is Cindy." The southern girl sounded nervous.

"How ya doin'? How did it go with the so-called client?" Maggie immediately switched to her Cindy matching accent.

"Not good. I need to see you. I need to talk to you."

"You can come over. I was just gettin' ready for beddy-bye."

"Much obliged. Where do you live?"

"I live at The Diplomat on Twelfth Street, number 321."

Cindy finished, "Thank you, I know where that is. I'll be there soon."

Maggie got into a long, yellow-flowered flannel nightgown. She laid on her bed to read the horror novel *Cujo* by Steven King. When the doorbell rang, she got up to let her friend in.

Maggie said, "What happened to you? You look as white as a ghost, and what's with the dark glasses?"

Cindy was still wearing her escort clothes. She was in a red mini-dress designed to show as much leg as possible. She wore three-inch red heels. Big dark glasses covered some of her face.

She took off the glasses revealing a big black-and-blue left eye.

"Who did this?" Maggie asked. "Who hit you?"

Cindy started to cry while talking, "When I was with the client tonight, Jake went to a bar across the street from the hotel. When I was done with the client, he came to get me at the room. He was drunk. I said I should drive because of his condition. Then he hit me in the face."

"That guy is a bastard."

"It gets worse. He had a baseball bat. He hit me with it five times, hard. Then he forced me onto the bed, and raped me."

Maggie hugged her crying friend and had her sit down on the couch. She said, "This guy is toast."

"Bonnie, I'm scared. I don't know what to do. Should I go to the cops?"

"No cops. I'll take care of this. The cops will just let him off scott-free and blame it on you. I hate rapists and woman beaters, and this guy is both. I have some experience with this kind of thing. I'll handle it my way. I just need a few days to get some stuff."

"Bonnie, what can you do? He's a big, mean, strong man."

"Any man that beats and rapes women is a coward. You'd be surprised at what a woman can do when she puts her mind on it."

"Thank you, Bonnie. I've only known you for a couple of weeks. I'm so glad that I met you."

"You stay here tonight. You know, I just might take Jake up on his offer to work for him. I could use some fast money. Give me his phone number." Maggie stood up, "Yes Cindy, Bonnie Dickerson is going to try her luck as a professional female escort."

Maggie met with Jake Boras at the Little Miss Whiskey's Country Bar on Sunday night. They sat in a booth away from the loud dance floor so they could talk.

Jake bought Maggie a Coke. "You're making a great decision here, Bonnie. You are going to make a great addition to my collection of female specimens."

"I need some fast money. When do I start?" Maggie asked with her country accent.

"This Wednesday. I got a longtime client. I would say that he is my best client. Mr. Selbourne has been married for twenty some years. He wants this to be extremely discreet."

"I can tell ya, Jake, nobody anywhere is more discreet than me."

Jake continued, "He pays in cash. I usually charge five hundred dollars. I told him he was getting a special new girl, so I got an extra hundred out of him."

"How much do I get?"

"If all goes well, you get two hundred."

Maggie smiled at Jake. "Woo-wee! That's a lot of money."

"Go to this motel at 7 p.m." Jake handed her a piece of paper. "I won't be able to go with you. I have some business to take care of. If anything goes wrong, call me at my office. I know you know what to do."

"Shucks, Jake. If there is anything Bonnie Dickerson knows, it's how to show a man a good time."

Maggie made the short drive back to her apartment. She would have Molly Jones call in sick for the next few days. That way she could continue as Bonnie. The plan was already set, and Jake Boras would have quite a Wednesday night this week.

On Monday morning Maggie started to get ready for her day. She called in sick, but still got dressed in a dull-green business suit. She put her dark-brown La Belle Époque wig on over her tight wig-cap. She used her fingers to remove the blue contact lenses. She replaced them with dark brown ones. Finally, she put on the brown full-rimmed glasses.

She looked at herself in a full-length mirror. She said in a nasally voice, "Yes, yes. It looks like Molly Jones is ready for some good shopping, very good."

Maggie had to drive east into Maryland to get to the store she desired. It was in the city of Bowie, Maryland, about a two-hour drive from DC. She hoped that they would have everything she needed at the Sportsman's Emporia.

Maggie entered the rather large store and started to browse the merchandise. There were guns of every kind, hunting supplies, fishing supplies, just about anything a sportsman would want or need. She found a display with the first thing on her shopping list.

A rugged looking grey-haired man approached her. "Can I help you miss?"

Maggie replied nasally, "That's Ms. sir. Yes, yes. Need help. I want two of those." She pointed at the display.

"That's our best model. It comes with a lifetime guarantee."

"Best is good. Guarantee is good, very good. I want two of them. I also need a good hunting knife and some bullets. Do you have rope? I need very strong rope."

The salesman asked, "This is for your husband, right Ms.? You don't look like a hunter."

"No, no. No husband. I am a very avid hunter. I need three boxes of 38 special ammunition, a twelve-inch spear-pointed hunting knife, and twenty yards of nylon rope, one inch in diameter. Do you have a book on how to tie knots?"

On the drive home Maggie felt very satisfied with her day. She found all she needed in one place. Just two days of planning and practice and she would be ready for her big date Wednesday night.

Hotel Six could have been called the Hotel Sex, but Maggie noted that it wasn't too seedy or too old. It was just seedy enough for this kind of activity. Maggie went to the front desk and asked for a reservation under Jake Boras. She asked for a room on the first floor in the back end of the motel. "Make sure it's the quietest room you have," she said as she winked at the front-desk attendant. She took her large suitcase and walked down the hall. She came to room 130. She opened the door with her key.

There was a king-size bed, a small desk and chair, and a black and white TV. Maggie didn't want to start setting up yet. In the mirror, Maggie saw a young girl with a yellow mini-dress that was designed to show as much leg as possible. The pigtails were gone, and her blond hair was straight and long. She waited patiently for her date to arrive.

At 7:30 p.m. sharp, there was a knock on the door. Maggie got off the bed and opened it. In the doorway stood a little middle-aged man with a bouquet of twelve red carnations. He handed them to Maggie.

Seymore Selbourne said to Maggie as she closed the door, "My goodness, you are a prize. Just beautiful and well worth the extra money."

Seymore was six inches shorter than Maggie. He had a short, brown mustache with wire-rimmed glasses. He wore a brown suit with a red bow tie.

Maggie looked at Seymore. She lost the country accent and said, "You got to be kidding?" She threw the flowers on the desk.

"My name is Seymore, and you are?" his voice was almost as nasally as Molly's.

"I'm Debbie." She took his hand and sat down with him on the bed. "Let's get this over with."

Maggie stood up and turned around. She bent over and picked up the back of her dress. Seymore sat there with a blank look on his face.

Maggie turned around again and said, "Okay. That's all you get. You can leave now."

Seymore protested, "Leave now? No, I paid a lot of money for this. We are supposed to have sex."

Maggie laughed, "Me have sex with you? Haven't you noticed that you're just a little twit?"

"No, you are a prostitute. You give me sex for money."

Maggie faked anger. "Listen you little shit. I am not a prostitute. I am a female escort. When I took this job, I didn't see sex as part of the job description. You are so ugly, and you smell like the cheapest cologne ever made. You'd better go now."

"This is not right by any means. You can be sure I am going to complain quite loudly to Jake Boras. You will be fired." The little man tried to be firm.

"Listen twit, why don't you complain to him right now."

Maggie dialed the phone. "Jake, this is Bonnie. We got a problem here with this guy. You talk to him."

Maggie handed the phone to Seymore. "Jake? This is Mr. Selbourne. I am very, very unhappy with the service of this woman. She will not have sex with me, and she keeps calling me names. She calls me a twit. I most definitely will have to ask for my money back."

Maggie took the phone from Seymore, "Jake, do you see what this twit is doing? I showed him my ass, and that's all he gets, and Jake, I want to get paid tonight. I want my two hundred dollars tonight."

Jake said, "Just wait there. I'll be there with the money within the hour."

Maggie put the phone down. She took her suitcase and opened it up on the bed. She took out her 38 special revolver and the hunting knife.

She pointed the gun at Seymore. "You'd better leave now. And one more thing, you should be ashamed of yourself. Carrying on like this when you have a wife of twenty years. She deserves better than you. I don't want to see you doing this again."

Seymore cried and ran to the door. "I'm so embarrassed," he said as he left the room.

Now Maggie could set up for the evening's festivities.

Maggie was ready and waiting. She had changed into some blue-denim jeans and a brown sweatshirt, and had on white sneakers. The last thing she did was unscrew all the lightbulbs in the room. She waited while her keen eyes adjusted to the darkness.

When Jake arrived, he opened the door of the room with his key. Maggie was crouched down by the wall near the open door. As he entered, she shut the door.

"Why is it so dark in...Oww!" he screamed violently as the sound of a loud snap reverberated through the room.

The screaming man bent over to grab his right shin. Maggie had the second bear trap resting on a small square of plywood. She moved it to where she thought his next left step would be. There was another loud snap as the springs in the trap closed the sharp jaws around his other shin.

The crouched-over man was desperately trying to remove the traps in the total darkness when Maggie jumped on his back and started choking him. The screaming man tried to get her off his back. She waited till she felt he was woozy, then she got off his back and took a large lasso with a noose-style knot and wrapped the noose around his body. When she pulled hard on the rope, the noosed tightened, pinning his arms against his sides. She ran around him in a counterclockwise direction over ten times making sure the rope was tight with every pass. Each time she passed his face, she punched it hard with her left hand.

Maggie pushed the screaming, tied up man onto the floor. She went to a lamp by the bed and screwed back in the bulb. The light came on and she took a strip of duct tape and stuck it over his bearded mouth to quiet him. She made sure all the knots of the rope were tight and secure.

"How's it going Jake?" Maggie dropped the southern accent. "Having a bad day? I see you brought your baseball bat. Were you going to use that on me?"

The duct-taped man was wide-eyed and staring at her. He nodded up and down yes, then back and forth, no.

With a smile she said, "I can tell you are so happy that I am one of your specimens. Am I right Jake?"

He shook his head back and forth, no.

Maggie continued, "Jake, I'm going to take this tape off. You know it is good thing for an employee and her boss to have a good heart-to-heart discussion now and then."

Maggie tore off the tape with one violent rip. "Now stay quiet, my pimp." She showed him her weapons. "I can go either way, gun, or knife. I just can't decide. A girl has so many tough choices to make nowadays."

With a crying whimper, Jake pleads, "Please don't hurt me. I give up."

"Here's the thing. I hate rapists and women beaters, and you are both. You raped and beat up my friend. I think I have two choices on what to do with you. I always think things through, and I have two choices.

Here they are:

CHOICE #1: Knife:

Cons: 1. Very slow and painful.

        2. Messy

        3. Too much screaming.

Pros: 1. Kills you.

        2. Much, Much pain.

        3. You don't hurt women ever again.

        4. Very slow and painful.

CHOICE #2: Gun:

Cons: 1. Too loud. Someone might hear.

        2. Messy.

        3. You die too fast.

Pros: 1. Kills you
2. I get out of here quicker.
3. I don't have to stab your stinking guts."

Jake tried to plead, "It's the alcohol. The alcohol made me do it."

"No excuse, Jake. You seem to be crying too much for a tough-ass pimp. I think you're more like a limp-assed wimp. Either way, I have made my choice. Since 'very slow and painful' appears in both the pros and cons of knife, I choose knife."

"Please don't kill me. My mom needs me," the crying Jake said. "She is very old and frail."

"Jake, do you live with your Mommy?"

"Yes, and she loves me."

"Touching, Jake, you know a woman's work is never done. Now I have another choice to make.

CHOICE #1: I kill you. Then you can never rape or beat a woman again.

CHOICE #2: I can cut off your cock. Then you can never rape a woman again, but you can still beat them."

"I won't do it again, I promise."

Maggie said, "I think I'm going with #2." Maggie unbuckled his belt and took down his pants.

"No, please! Don't cut it off."

"You know Jake, I sanitized this knife with vodka. It is going to be a very sanitary and clean surgical procedure. I only have two choices, Jake."

"No." he begged. "I have a third choice."

Maggie laughed, "You do? This is very good Jake. We are two adults discussing our options. What is it?"

"You can let me go. My Mommy loves me."

"So, I should untie you, take off your bear trap shoes, and let you go?"

"Yes."

"I'm going with choice number four. I'm going to take off the bear traps and take them with me. You never know when a girl might need a bear trap in the city. I am going to leave you tied up. The cleaning lady will find you in the morning."

"Thank you, Bonnie," the sobbing Jake said.

"Shut up. If you ever hurt another woman again, I will know. I will come back. It will make this night seem like a day at Disneyland. I will cut off your cock and several other appendages you have."

Maggie removed the traps from his shins, packed up, and left the room.

The following Saturday, Cindy called up Maggie. She sounded excited. "Bonnie, can we meet tonight at Little Whiskey's? I have some great news."

"Love to hear it, girl," Maggie said with her thick country drawl. "Be there at eight."

They met at the same booth that Maggie met with Jake. It was a little quieter.

Cindy was gushing. "That moron Jake called me yesterday. He tried to apologize for what he did to me."

Maggie said, "He's a jerk. I told you I would handle it."

"I don't know about that, but that's not the news."

"So, what's up girl?"

"I got a call from a bank. They said someone set up a trust fund for me. It's a bunch of dough. I can only use it for my education."

"So how much? Maggie asked.

"It's enough for me to go back to the University of North Carolina."

"So you can become a one of those big city lawyers?"

"Bonnie, it's even more than that. There's enough there for graduate school. I really want to be the best lawyer."

Maggie said, "Let's get out of here. I'm getting tired of this place."

They both walked out of the club and toward the parking lot. It was a wonderful DC night. There were no clouds in the late-night sky. The cool summer wind warmed their bodies.

Cindy said, "I don't know who did this. The only clue I have is that it is somebody named Maggie."

"Who's Maggie?" Maggie asked.

"I have no idea."

"Maybe you have a long-lost rich aunt that left you this money?"

"Bonnie, I don't have a relative named Maggie."

Maggie said back, "Whoever this Maggie is, she must have much love for you. I have to go Cindy. I see a friend."

"Later, girl"

Maggie rushed to the trench coat and fedora-wearing man leaning on her car. "Hello Lawrence." Maggie took his arm and led him away from the car. "See, I can feel you. You're not a ghost, you're an angel."

The Inspector said back, "No, I get to take human, not angel form, when I perform these inspections."

"So, how did you get to become an Inspector?"

"It was an exceptionally long time ago, Maggie. Over two thousand years ago."

"I didn't think they wore fedoras two thousand years ago."

"I didn't have this look then. I picked it up in the 1930's."

"I must say, it makes you look kind of handsome for a guy in his two-thousands."

The Inspector smiled. "Flattery will get you nowhere, Maggie."

"Anyway, I did rather good this time. I didn't kill that raping, woman-beating bastard. I didn't even cut off his cock."

"You were very compassionate, Maggie. You helped your friend, then you left that idiot in the hotel room, tied up with his pants down. You should have seen the look on the cleaning ladies' face when she found him."

"Was it funny? I couldn't hang around."

"Even us Angels need a laugh now and then."

He put his hand on Maggie's forehead.

Maggie's mind exploded.

XI. THE ANGEL

Maggie was always way too clever to ever get caught at any of her crimes. The authorities that investigated these crimes never had a clue as to who she was. No fingerprints, no birth records, and no hospital or school records. How can they investigate a person that does not exist? Of course, we know she exists. Yes, and I believe everyone reading this journal knows she does exist.

There was one small mistake she made. I believe one lucky French detective found something from a crime she committed years before. This could not possibly plague Maggie for even a short time. Remember who we are dealing with here. I heard there was a trial or maybe it was a hearing. Was it for murder? Maybe for computer hacking? I thought I saw once that she got a parking ticket.

Anyway, the Consul is back, and they want to see more. I think all the Beings in the Bliss want to see more.

I am going to dive in and examine this so-called trial of Maggie Love.

11. In Her Sixties

MAGGIE WOKE UP.

She was in a bed somewhere, but she did not know where. There was too much spinning, too much blurry murkiness, too much insane driving pain in her head. She tried to get out of bed and was thrown to the floor by something that felt like a major earthquake. Only this earthquake tilted the room by 180 degrees putting the floor where the ceiling should be and the ceiling replacing the floor.

Maggie stayed on the floor above until the spinning reversed the upside-down room back to its normal position. She tried not to throw up as the nausea started to conquer her entire body. The pounding in her head was loud and violent.

As the spinning started to slowly calm down, she realized the pounding was not in her head, but was coming from the front door of her apartment. The blurriness was almost gone when she saw her door crash open. First, one policeman entered with a handgun, pointing it at every direction. Soon, two more police followed mimicking the same motions as the first. They were all navigating the apartment using the French language to communicate.

When the first officer got to Maggie's bedroom, he pointed the gun at the woman on the floor and said in French, *"Don't move."*

"What do you men want? I hope you have a warrant to come in here," Maggie said from the floor.

A tall, thin man in a dark suit with a red necktie pushed his way through his men. His hair was brown with grey around the sides. His beady eyes made him look a little scary. He looked down on Maggie and said, *"We don't need a search warrant here in France. Are you Susan Grey, my dear? And why are you on the floor?"*

"I might be Susan Grey. I got dizzy when I woke up. All the pounding startled me. Is it 5:30 in the morning?"

"Yes Madam. I have been looking for you for a long time Susan, some ten years now. I was so anxious to meet you, we came in early."

"I'm at a disadvantage, sir?" Maggie asked.

The man in the suit said, "I am so sorry Madam, I am Lieutenant Beaumont of The French National Police. It is not very lady-like to be drunk from wine this early in the morning, Susan." He turned to his men. "Help the fine lady up."

Two of the policemen helped Maggie up. She said to them, "So, to what do I owe this pleasurable visit?"

Lieutenant Beaumont said with a big smile, "I am putting you under arrest for murder. Let me read you your rights. You have the right to notify a relative and/or an employer. Since you are an American, you have the right to notify consular authorities at the United States Embassy. You have the right to be examined by a doctor. You have the right to an attorney. You have the right to an interpreter if needed. I do not think you need this, Miss Grey. You have the right to see certain documents on the procedure against you. And you have the right to make statements to the public prosecutor deciding on your continued custody. And finally, you have the right to make statements, answer questions, or remain silent."

Maggie replied, "That's quite a mouthful Lieutenant. Do I have the right to get dressed? Or do I have to go in my nighty?"

"We have a female officer, Officer Fulford. She will frisk you and help you prepare for your little trip."

"So, Sargent Beaumont, why are you picking on an old lady like me? Who did I kill and when?" Maggie asked with a smile.

Beaumont said harshly, "It is Lieutenant, and at first this case was ruled as a suicide. I did the forensics at the original crime scene. I knew better. I am arresting you for the murder of Paul Dubois ten years ago on February 12, 2009."

○‿○

Maggie sat in the back seat of the French police car with handcuffs on and the female officer sitting next to her. It was about an eighteen-kilometer drive to the 8th Arrondissement Police Station. Maggie wasn't scared or nervous.

The *déjà vu* in her head was overwhelming, and she knew everything was going exactly as planned. Doing this again was going to be so much fun.

She said to the Lieutenant in the front passenger seat, in her perfect French, "*Hey Captain, I am going to need a lawyer.*"

The lieutenant turned around and said, "*It is Lieutenant, and you are seriously going to need a lawyer, Miss Grey. You are seriously going to need one.*"

"One more question? Maggie asked. "*What is the date?*"

Officer Fulford replied, "*It is March 3rd.*"

"*The year?*" Maggie asked impatiently.

"*You did have too much wine, Miss Grey.*" The lieutenant laughed. "*It is 2019.*"

❦

The interrogation room was small and dimly lit. There was a small indiscreet white table in the middle with three chairs. Maggie sat on one side of the table. On the other side sat Lieutenant Frank Beaumont and Officer Maria Fulford.

"*I hope you're the bad cop, Officer Fulford. Lieutenant Beaumont looks both mean and ugly. If he is the bad cop, I think I'm in trouble,*" Maggie coolly said.

The Lieutenant leaned close to Maggie. "*We don't play that good cop/bad cop here. We just put murderers away for good.*"

"*You know I'm not saying anything, and I want a lawyer.*"

Officer Fulford said, "*We need a DNA sample, Miss Grey.*" The officer handed Maggie a cotton swab. "*Just rub this between your cheek and gums.*"

Maggie did so. She looked at Beaumont. "*You know, if you think I did this, you must be the stupidest detective in all of France.*"

He answered her, "*I have tons of circumstantial evidence and a witness, and I recently found one more thing. Our forensic team was able to carefully remove the dried blood from the murder weapon. We found a small brown hair in the dried blood. We will soon have your DNA. I know it will be a match.*"

Maggie said, "*I want a lawyer, Detective. Or should I call you little douchebag?*"

In a whisper the detective ordered his officer to stand behind her and block the camera.

He leaned even closer to Maggie. He made a honking sound and spit in her face. "*That's what I think of murdering bitches. I think you killed many more than this one. Why don't you just confess?*"

"Listen little douchey, spit all you want. I need my lawyer."

"Get her out of here!" the detective yelled.

Officer Fulford handed Maggie a small handkerchief. Maggie wiped the spit off her face and hid the rag in the palm of her hand. As the officer escorted her out of the room, Maggie thought to herself, "That was way too easy. I thought I might have to scratch him or something. Now we are even. He has mine, and I have his."

They put Maggie in a small room with a push-button phone on the wall. She dialed the number. After three beeps she heard a female voice speaking French, "*This is Cindy Taylor.*"

She said in her most southern accent, "Guess who this is?"

"Okay, kiddo. Where are you?" Cindy joined in with the same accent.

"The 8th Arrondissement Police Station. You know what time it is, don't ya?"

"What time is it?"

Maggie said in her most southern drawl, "It's showtime, girl!"

The two women entered a small room with only two chairs. There were no cameras, and the room was totally soundproof.

As they sat down, Maggie's lawyer said, "Hello Susan. I got you out on bail. There are some complications. The judge and prosecutor think you are a flight risk. You will be confined to your apartment complex, and you will have to wear an ankle monitor until conclusion of the trial."

Maggie smiled, "How fun! I get to wear a tracking device."

"Susan, depending on the results of the DNA test, they don't have much. They have some bad circumstantial evidence and some testimony from a Dubois. He was young at the time of the murder. His testimony is a little confused. These are things we can beat. The DNA will be the tough one."

"It's so good to see you Cindy. How's it going with that new boyfriend?"

"It's going good. We are talking about moving in together," Cindy got frustrated. "What am I talking about? Susan, I just saw you last week, but then you were Bonnie Dickerson. We need to talk about your case."

XI. THE ANGEL • 11. In Her Sixties

Maggie said quietly, "Keep it down Cindy." She talked loudly again, "Moving in together. That's great. This relationship is moving lightning fast."

"Well, you know, I am coming off that tough divorce ten months ago. Isn't that crazy? We met at a French café. There I go again. Shouldn't we talk about your case? You are in big trouble girl."

Maggie whispered, "Not here. I think this room is bugged." She spoke up, "Congrats, you passed the French bar. Now you can be my lawyer, and that is amazing."

Cindy said to her friend, "What's amazing is that you taught me French in just two months, so I could pass it."

"I am so thankful you came to help me. How much to do you charge?"

"I was retired. You invited me to Paris after my divorce. You paid all my expenses for ten months in Paris, and you're also the Maggie Lo…"

Maggie covered Cindy's mouth with her hand, she whispered firmly, "Never say that name around me in public."

"Okay, but we're not in public. If you are the Maggie that paid for my education, I'm not charging you anything."

"No, you're not doing that. You're getting' paid girl. How much is the bail?"

Cindy said, "Its steep, 500 hundred thousand euros."

"I told you how to get a cashier's check?"

"For some reason, I didn't think the money would be a problem," Cindy said.

Maggie stood up and proclaimed, "This is great. For the first time I get to see you work. I hope you don't charge me too much. I want a speedy trial."

Cindy complained, "Susan, I need time to prepare. These are profoundly serious charges. It's premeditated murder."

"Cindy my girl, you hardly have to do anything."

"Okay, 'Miss Think You're a Lawyer Girl,' why don't I have to do much work?"

Maggie said with confidence, "Because I already have this thing beat."

⁓⁓⁓

Cindy took Maggie back to her apartment in her red BMW5 series. Cindy wore a dark- brown business suit, and her hair was recently dyed black. Her sixty-five years was starting to show, but her aging face made her look smart and sophisticated.

Maggie had just hit sixty-three, and she fared much better. Her long hair was straight and brown with streaks of silver. The tanned skin on her face was soft and firm. If you looked closely you might find one or two wrinkles, but you had to really look for those.

Maggie said to Cindy, "Did you bring me what I asked for?"

"The bag is in the back seat."

Maggie reached back to retrieve it.

Cindy told her, "They searched your place. All they took was your computer."

"Perfect," Maggie said. "That was not really my computer."

"Don't tell me."

Maggie pulled a three-inch-thick, eighteen by eighteen-inch tablet out of the small light brown bag. She showed it to Cindy. "This is. It's a mini super-computer."

When they arrived at the apartment complex, they were greeted at the front gate by Officer Fulford and another male police officer. She said to Maggie, *"I have a present for you Miss Grey. Once inside your place, I will give it to you."*

Maggie's apartment was simply decorated with not much flash or flare. It was a one- bedroom with a living area, a kitchen, and a small bathroom. Officer Fulford told Maggie to sit down on the couch and to take off her right shoe and sock. Fulford strapped a black band around Maggie's ankle. Attached to the band was a black oval mechanism about five inches by two inches.

When all was complete the officer said, *"All right Miss Grey, the CWG international tracking bracelet is applied and activated. If you leave the apartment complex, we will know and we will find you. If you try to take it off, again we will find you, and we will arrest you. Both would be a violation of your bail agreement, and then we will take you to jail."*

Maggie stood up and showed her ankle to her lawyer Cindy. She said in French, *"What do you think Cindy? I don't think black is my color."* She turned to Officer Fulford, *"Do you have it in yellow?"*

"No Miss Grey, we do not have it in yellow. Just behave yourself until the trial. Hopefully, I won't see you until then."

The two officers left the apartment leaving Cindy and Maggie alone.

Cindy said, "Now can we finally discuss your case?"

"Can we meet tomorrow at 9 a.m.? I have some work to do. I can't believe you're my lawyer. Sleep tight Cindy Taylor.

Cindy said back, "Sleep tight Bonnie, I mean Mag, whoops, I mean Susan. Damn, I don't even know what the hell to call you."

Maggie looked at her watch. It was 8:50 in the morning. She still had ten minutes until her meeting with Cindy. She jogged to the main gate of the apartment complex and opened it up with her key card. She started to jog up the stairs to the third floor when her iPhone sang a song. She answered it.

"I'm here Susan," The voice on the other end said.

Maggie answered, "I'll be right there. I still got five minutes."

They met at her front door, and Maggie opened it.

Maggie said to Cindy as they sat down on the couch, "I skipped breakfast today. I am going to be hungry soon. I found a great new Chinese place; they open at eleven. Do you want to go there, or should we order in?"

Maggie was wearing pink jogging shorts with a dark-blue sweatshirt. She had yellow Nike Zoom Fly running shoes. Cindy noticed her bare ankle.

"Susan where's the ankle monitor?" Cindy was concerned. "I swear they are going to come here any minute and take you to jail."

"Cindy, remember when I told you that you can only call me Maggie when we are alone? I checked this place for bugs. There are none."

"Okay Maggie, where the hell is the ankle monitor?"

"It's on my desk, next to my computer."

The two got up and walked to Maggie's desk. The monitor was there, and the mechanism was opened.

Cindy said in a panic, "Okay, I'll think of something to say when the authorities get here. I know, you had an allergic reaction to the leather strap."

"Cindy, I took it off last night. I just took a five-mile run around the neighborhood."

"What did you do to it? The monitor?" Cindy asked.

Maggie took her into her bedroom. On the floor next to the bed was something that looked like a sleeping bag. Maggie picked it up.

"I'm really scared of EMF, that's electromagnetic fields. With cell phones and Wi-Fi and such, it's everywhere, so I bought this online about a year ago. It is a Faraday Shield. It protects you from all those rays, and I enhanced this one. It is also highly effective at stopping those rays from leaving it."

They went back to the computer. "So how did you get it off? The band isn't even cut or damaged."

"That was easy. I am very flexible. From inside of the shield, I heated the band slightly and used some butter for grease. I stretched my foot straight like a ballerina. It slid right off."

"Maggie, I don't recommend this behavior."

"Here is the best part. See this SIM card in my computer?"

"Sure."

"I took it out of the ankle monitor. I can use it with an app to simulate my movement around the apartment. I can simulate exercise, sleep, or movement around the complex. They will never know. I'm going to order Chinese, then we can start our meeting."

Maggie came back into the living room, and the two women sat down on the couch. Maggie spoke first. "So, you are officially my lawyer. Here in France, we have professional secrecy."

"That's right Maggie. Everything we talk about is kept a total secret between us."

"So, are you going to ask me if I killed that bastard?"

"I don't need to ask that now. I need to ask where you were the day Paul Dubois was murdered."

"Just ask." Maggie insisted.

"Okay, did you kill him?"

Maggie answered immediately, "Of course I did, and the old man deserved it."

"Maggie you can't be judge and jury in this. That is not a defense."

"I was still worried about this place being bugged when I wrote this last night." Maggie handed her a stack of papers. Each page was filled with beautifully perfect cursive handwriting. "You read this while I make us a high-protein smoothie."

As Cindy read, her eyes got bigger and bigger. She started flipping through the pages faster and faster. There were a few gasps as her mouth was now wide open. She stood up and read the last pages as she walked toward the kitchen. When she got there, the sound of the blender turning on startled her. The pages flew out of her hands all over the floor. The two women bent down to pick them up.

Facing Maggie while crouched down, Cindy said with a shaky voice, "All this can't be true. Tell me you just have a wild imagination."

"It's all true, Cindy."

"You have killed eighteen people?"

Maggie stood up. She took all the pages and went to her gas stove. She turned on the stove and ignited a corner of the stack of papers. She put them in the sink and let them burn up.

"Eighteen if you count my mom. But she made me do it, and she trained me to do it. Killing you own mom can really mess up a youngster's head, lawyer girl. Men don't treat us women with any respect, and when they do this, I take the law into my own hands. I can tell you, they all deserved it."

Cindy stood beside her client. "But you did kill one woman. She seemed to be totally innocent."

"I do regret that. Veronica was collateral damage, and I was so young at the time. Well, are you still my lawyer?"

"Of course. It doesn't concern me about your past, even if it is all true. I am defending you against these present charges and these charges only."

"That's the way, girl. When is the speedy trial?"

Maybe two weeks, maybe three."

Maggie gave her a slight smile, "Let's meet in a couple of days. You look kind of pale."

"Perfect. I have lots of work to do. We should have the DNA results by then. Maggie, you allegedly did this because they deserved it?"

"Yes, of course they did. But it is more than that."

"What do you mean, more?"

"It's not easy being Maggie Love."

※

"*I got the results Lieutenant.*" Officer Fulford entered the prosecutor's small office.

Sitting behind the desk in the center was Attorney Joseph Fontaine, a blond man with the look of a championship French cyclist. He was young and full of ambition and his goal was to make France the safest country in the world. Across from him sat the Detective Lieutenant Beaumont. Fulford sat down in a chair next to the Lieutenant. She put the report on the desk and said, *"It is something. I'm not sure it's enough."*

The lieutenant spoke, *"Just give it to me like it is."*

"The sample was small, old, and damaged. The result is that there is a 28 percent chance that the DNA is that of Susan Grey."

Beaumont asked the prosecutor, *"That should be enough, right Joseph?"*

He answered, *"For your sake, I hope so. We have invested so much time and money in this already. Tell me about the witness you have."*

"His name is Clement Dubois, now sixteen years old. He is the great grandnephew of the victim. He was six years old at the time of the murder. He might be a little confused at times, but he does remember his father constantly talking about a witch named Mademoiselle Amour. He thinks he saw her once. I have convinced him, when he is questioned by the judge, to be absolutely positive about the sighting. His description of this Mademoiselle matches Susan Grey."

"Where is the father?"

Beaumont answered, *"Deceased. I think this Grey was responsible for his demise also."*

"One at a time, Lieutenant. Who is representing Grey?" the attorney asked.

"She is an American lawyer, named Cinthia Tailor. She just passed the French bar."

"Has she ever represented anyone in France before?

"No, this is her first French case. Although she does have twenty-plus years of criminal lawyer experience in the United States."

The prosecutor looked hard at the two police officers. *"That might work to our advantage. We are going to move on with this. You'd better pray that the Judge President does not throw this case out. If he does, you will be writing parking tickets for the rest of your careers."*

<hr />

Maggie was looking forward to her meeting with her lawyer, Cindy. She was coming over at 11:30 a.m. At 11:20 the doorbell rang. Maggie ran to the door and opened it.

"Come in, girl."

Maggie was wearing jogging shorts with a white tank top. She had on yellow socks.

"Hello Maggie," Cindy looked at her ankle. "As your lawyer, I would feel a lot better if you put that ankle device back on. You already proved you could beat it."

"But Cindy, I like to take my morning run."

"Run around the complex, please Maggie. You never know when the police might show up."

"Okay, scaredy cat, but I know when they are coming."

"How? They took away your internet."

"Sorry, Cindy. They did not. Let me show you."

The two walked over to the desk with the computer tablet sitting on top. Maggie turned it on, "There is a special Wi-Fi that few know about. There are only fourteen of us that can access it. The signal comes from a satellite that is connected to a very special and powerful server. It takes twenty minutes just to get in. There is a complex series of passwords, motions, and tap sequences. If you mess up, you get one more chance. Mess-up again and you're out. We change it every week."

Cindy asked, "Who's the 'we'?

"We are members of HWN, The World Hacking Network. We are more interested in knowledge than applying viruses or trolling. I do know some members have fattened their bank accounts."

"Is that how you got so rich?"

"No Cindy. I just use it for learning and fun, and I am going to have fun in the next few days. Are you hungry? I ordered Chinese."

Suddenly, the doorbell rang. Maggie opened a drawer on the desk and took out a plastic bag.

"Is the Chinese food here already?"

Maggie laughed, "It's not the Chinese."

She opened her front door and was greeted by a young dark and handsome Frenchman. He said with a big smile, *"Mademoiselle, it is so good to see you."*

"Yes, me too Felipe, and thank you for helping me again," She handed him the plastic bag. *"You know where to take it? Right away now."*

"Yes, Mademoiselle, just like you told me."

Maggie handed Felipe an envelope full of euros, and he scooted away.

She returned to the couch, and the two sat down.

Cindy said, "I'm your lawyer. You are supposed to tell me everything. Why did you just give that guy a tampon in a zip lock bag? I think you're done with menopause."

"Maybe, and you know I'm into women's rights. I think they might be putting something in those things that's harmful. He's taking it to a lab to have it analyzed."

"Okay, so you wanted a speedy trial. We have ten days. You got to give me something. Do you have an alibi?"

Maggie laughed again, "Of course not, Cindy. I was there."

"I know that, I think. Now make something up. They have a weak case. The DNA came back with a 28 percent chance that it is yours. They have a witness that was six years old at the time. He slightly remembers a Mademoiselle Amour, and she was with a black guy. The witness is a relative of the deceased. He is sixteen now. His name is Clement Dubious. Remember Maggie, in France I cannot cross examine the witness. The only one that can question him is the judge."

"Oh yes, the black guy is James. I remember we did see this kid briefly ten years ago. But that was a different murder. The kid thought I was a witch, and I heard he is also kind of stupid."

The doorbell rang. Maggie got up to get it. "The Chinese is here. Don't worry Cindy, I will work on the alibi, and I will come up with something about the witness. But this thing is not going to last that long."

"How do you know that, 'Miss Think You're a Lawyer Girl'?"

"How many times do I have to say it? I got his beat already. I do need you to do one thing."

"What's that?"

"One day before the trial starts, ask them to recheck the DNA evidence. We have that right."

Cindy shook her head and said, "Whatever."

⁂

The streets of Paris were always narrow and mostly full of small cars. The traffic was worse on this particular day as a steady rain fell over the city. The beautiful old architecture that surrounded them made the drive to the courthouse seem serene and cool, and Maggie was loving the Paris ambiance. It filled her with peace.

Maggie sat in the police van with Cindy by her side. Next to her was Officer Fulford. A large policeman was driving the van. Next to him in the passenger seat sat Lieutenant Beaumont.

Maggie broke the silence. *"I'm glad you took that bracelet off. It was getting so annoying."*

"Not for long. I will put it back on after today's proceedings," the officer said back.

Beaumont said from the front seat, "*You know, Miss Grey, since you are technically a prisoner of the court, we can assign two guards to sit with you. Officer Fulford and I volunteered for the job. I want to see you put away up close.*"

Maggie sounded enthusiastic. *"How fun. You can keep me company, and I get to see you up close when we make a fool out of you."*

The Detective sneered, "*You seem awful confident for someone that's going to jail for the rest of your life.*"

The courtroom was old and smelled of mahogany. Shiny polished wood was everywhere. The lights were dim, giving the room an historically ancient feel.

Maggie sat above the courtroom in a box behind her lawyer with Lieutenant Beaumont on her right and Officer Fulford to her left. Cindy Tailor, seated a few feet below Maggie, had hired two paralegals that sat on each side of her. Across the courtroom was the prosecutor's table. The *General Avocat* Joseph Fontaine looked fidgety and nervous. In front of him was a jury of six. The audience in the back was full. This did not please Maggie. She did not want the publicity.

As the three judges entered the courtroom, everyone stood. The Judge *Président* was wearing a red and white robe with a gold and white sash over his shoulder. The two associate judges on each side of him wore black robes. The Judge *Président* looked much older and wiser than the two associates.

Fontaine quickly approached the high bench where the three judges sat. He talked softly to the judges, so no one could hear. The judge then motioned to Cindy to approach the bench. During this small conference, Joseph Fontaine was waving his arms around radically as if to make a worthless point.

Maggie whispered to the Lieutenant, *"That prosecutor looks as nervous as a long-tailed cat in a room full of rocking chairs."*

The Lieutenant shot back, *"I don't know what's going on, but something is going on."*

Two lawyers returned to their seats. Cindy stared at Maggie with her eyes wide open, as the Judge *Président* banged his gavel. He spoke in a low, scratchy voice into a microphone, *"It seems there was a mistake made. I need to hear more. I call to the stand, Camille LeBlanc."*

An extremely skinny, short woman with coke-bottle glasses quickly approached the small wooden fence in front of the judge. There were tears in her eyes.

The Judge President asked, *"You are Camille LeBlanc?"*

She spoke into the microphone in front of her, *"Yes, Monsieur le Président."*

"And what do you do?"

"I am the Director of DNA research at the National Police Crime Lab."

"Explain to me how a mistake like this could be made?"

Camille was having trouble holding back the tears. *"I don't know. We rechecked the data and got a different result. I checked it four times, and I had two colleagues check it also. It was always the same. There is 0 percent chance that the DNA from the hair sample belongs to Susan Grey."*

The courtroom erupted with gasps and loud murmurs from all over the room.

The judge banged his gavel to quiet everyone down. He spoke harshly to the crying woman, *"How could this be? All this time and money wasted. Not to mention the embarrassment to the defendant, Miss Grey."*

"I am so sorry Monsieur le Président; we will go over our standard operating procedures to make sure this never happens again. If it is any consolation, we ran the DNA through our database again and we got a 99.9 percent match."

"I am not sure I should ask this, but I will. Who is the match?"

Camille got control of her tears, then strongly said, *"The DNA on the hair found under the blood of the knife used to murder Paul Dubois belongs to Lieutenant Frank Beaumont of the National Police."*

The courtroom erupted in loud yells and gasps. People stood up and watched with amazement. The judge banged his gavel hard and long to quiet the court.

XI. THE ANGEL • 11. In Her Sixties

Lieutenant Beaumont stood up and yelled over the noise, *"Of course it could be my DNA. I led the team that did the forensics at the original crime scene."*

As the room quieted, Camille said into the microphone, *"That is true, but our crime lab has determined that the hair was on the knife before the murder."*

The room erupted again. The Judge President banged his gavel then said, *"The court offers our sincere apology to Miss Susan Grey. You are free to go. Take Lieutenant Beaumont into custody for questioning. This trial is closed."*

As Officer Fulford led the protesting Beaumont away, Cindy Tailor turned around and looked up at Maggie with her eyes and mouth open.

Maggie smiled big and wide, she said in her most southern drawl, "Didn't I tell ya, girl? Now would ya please the court and take me to that there airport?"

―――

The rain again slowed their drive to Charles de Gaulle Airport. The traffic was stop and go. Cindy Tailor did not mind. She needed to talk to Maggie, "You asked me to keep in touch with your sister Laura, and I did. I wanted to wait until after the trial to tell you this. Your mother died last week."

Maggie didn't cry. "I know that. I would have gone back to California, but it's hard to travel when you're on trial for murder."

"So, you didn't shoot your mother."

"I sure did. Sally was my foster mother. She never believed that I shot my real mother. Though I know deep down inside, she did know. This amazing woman got me though that. She was always by my side."

There was a long period of silence, then Cindy asked, "How did you do it Maggie? That shit I saw in the court does not just happen.

Maggie smiled. "We still have that secrecy thing, right?"

"Of course."

"That bastard Beaumont spit in my face during our first interview. They gave me a hankie to wipe it off. I had to make sure I had that spit when I checked out of jail."

"How did you do that?"

"I asked for a Tampon. They never questioned the fact that I'm sixty-three."

"That's because you look like you're forty."

"I threw the Tampon away and stuffed the hankie inside the case. When I checked out of jail, they let me take it with me."

"So, the guy at your house was not taking the Tampon to a lab to analyze its ingredients."

"No, he was taking it to a lab that does DNA testing. It was easy to hack into their network and download the data on that cop. Much more difficult to get into the National Police network and find the so-called sample of my DNA."

"Perfect, you just pulled the old switcheroo."

"I did, and there's a bonus. I've been digging into police records and Beaumont's records. I found pretty some good evidence that Beaumont was in the back pocket of the Dubois clan. When they started dying, he was out big money. That is why he worked so long and so hard to find me."

"That's a bonus?"

"I planted some phony evidence that his deal with the Dubois went south. He was furious with them. Now he has a motive to knock them off."

"That's crazy. Let me ask you this: if you knew everything the police were doing, why didn't you just leave?"

"They wouldn't have let me leave, and besides I had to clear my name."

"But your name isn't even Susan Grey."

"I want all my aliases to have clear names."

"I'm afraid to ask this, but I will. How many aliases do you have?"

Maggie cracked up laughing, "Fourteen and counting."

The airport was busy and filled with people and cars racing around in circles. Cindy pulled over at the drop-off area at Terminal Two. As Maggie got out of the car, she noticed a man in a trench coat standing by the door. He was smoking a cigarette. Instantly, everything came back to her.

"Cindy, I have always had this strange feeling that the French Detective reminded me of some Inspector guy. Now I know why. I'm usually not a hugging person, but I'm going to make an exception today."

The two women hugged tightly, and Cindy said, "I feel so thankful today. It was amazing."

"Me too. Thank you so much for helping me. You know, I'm not going to be getting on that plane. That attorney Fontaine thinks I'm guilty. He had the doctor at the jail fake a diagnosis that I have Alzheimer's disease. They are going to put me in a home."

"I can get you out in hours. They have no right to do that."

"No need. I don't want any more publicity. I will escape in a matter of days and be home by the end of the week."

"I know I can't talk you out of it. So, I'm just going to say I'm thankful for that day I had in Washington DC some forty years ago."

"What happened then?"

"That was the day I met Maggie Love."

⁓

Maggie walked quickly to the airport entrance. She buzzed past the smoking man and said, "I'm tired of this shit, Inspector."

Inspector Lawrence threw his cigarette on the floor and stamped it out. He followed her inside.

He hustled to catch up with her and said from behind. "You think you're tired of this shit? I'm smoking two packs of those things a day since I met you. Wait up. You know you can't get away from me."

Maggie stopped, "Just kill me. I didn't hurt anyone this time. But you are going to kill me anyway, Angel Man."

The Inspector looked her in the eye. "No, you most probably put an innocent man in jail for the rest of his life. I think that's a crime. Look Maggie, just repent. Then we can end this—all of this."

"I can't do that. I lived my life my way, and everything I did was totally just. So just do it."

The Inspector took out a cigarette and lit it up inside the terminal. With a tear in his eye, he waved his hand.

Maggie's mind exploded.

XII. THE ANGEL

I QUIT. I CANNOT DO THIS ANYMORE. TWO THOUSAND YEARS OF THIS shit is enough. First the consul reprimands me because I was too harsh on Maggie. I agree that throwing her out of an airplane at ninety thousand feet above sea level is a little harsh. Maybe it is big-time harsh. So I try to be more compassionate with her. I spared her from going through a very difficult time in her life for the second time.

What do they do now? They reprimand me again, this time for going too easy on her and not finishing the bleak ordeal she was going through. It's enough to drive a sane Being totally insane. I must go through with this exam, and I must do as they ask. I still will never quit a job right in the middle of an examination.

But I promise you this. When this is done, I am going to quit this job and give the Consul a piece of my mind.

I will probably never do that. I just need to vent, to let off some steam, and you people are the only ones listening, so bear with me. This is what Maggie has done to me. Cigarettes, booze, screaming about The Consul, what's next? I haven't tried gambling yet. What I have to do next is not going to be easy.

I have to witness the near death of Maggie Love.

12. In Her Fifties

MAGGIE WOKE UP.

She was standing in a spinning, whirling room and nothing was discernible. Just unclear colors and the sound of a wind so strong that nothing else could be heard or seen. There was a foul smell of rotten almonds in the air and Maggie's instinct was to hold her breath to try to avoid the stinking gas. The spinning started to slow. She could see the outline of four men in front of her. She heard a voice scream out from one of the men in French, "*Frédéric was right. Maggie Love is a witch!*"

She heard four loud pops ring through the room and four powerful blows hitting her in the chest, throwing her two meters to the rear until she landed flat on her back. James and Bruce Cannon rushed to her side. Bruce put a gas mask over Maggie's face.

She pushed it away and tried not to breathe in. "Take me into our bedroom."

James said through the mask, "Maggie, there are gas canisters in there also."

Maggie said back, "Yes James, but those are filled with oxygen."

James picked Maggie up and carried her to the bedroom. Maggie had put the keypad locks on all the doors in the villa, and Bruce ran ahead of his parents, opening the bedroom door with the combination.

James gently put Maggie on the bed. Her shirt was stained in the middle of her chest with a growing spot of red blood.

Maggie kept repeating, "I will not go into shock. I will not go into shock. James, open my blouse. I will not go into shock."

James said to Bruce, "Bruce, call an ambulance. Your mom has been hit."

Maggie struggled to say, "Bruce, don't you dare! I'm not going into shock. I'm not going into shock."

James ripped the buttons off her blouse. "Maggie, you're wearing a bullet proof vest."

"I guess I didn't plan this well enough. I should have worn two because one damn bullet got through," Maggie voice was getting softer. "I'm not going into shock. I'm not going into shock. The bullet did not enter my heart. James, I have three antidote kits for the poison under the bed. All three of us will have to go through the procedure."

James took off his mask and kissed her cheek. He got close to her ear. "Maggie, we have to get you to a doctor."

"No doctors for Maggie Love. Bruce, keep your mask on. Go into the kitchen. Take knives, tweezers, scissors, and anything else we might need and boil them. Bring the first aid kit. I have some vodka in a top drawer in the kitchen. Bring it all."

"What about those guys out there?" Bruce asked.

Maggie tried to laugh through the pain. "Bruce, they're all dead by now. James you are going to get this bullet out of me."

"I can't Maggie. I'm no doctor."

"You can. It is not too deep. The vest slowed the bullet down. I will coach you through it. I will not go into shock. I will not go into shock. James, am I a witch like the Frenchman said?"

Maggie started to black out. She tried to use the power of her mind to stay awake. She used all the power of her intellect to stop her body and mind from going into shock.

"Get all the clean towels you can find James," Maggie said while gasping for air.

James soon returned with a stack of white towels.

"Put one on the wound, James. Apply all the pressure you can. You must slow the bleeding. Better yet, use your knee. Use all your body weight to apply all the pressure you can."

As James did this, Maggie cried out in agonizing pain. Bruce came back into the bedroom with the first-aid kit, the vodka, and the sterilized tools.

When Maggie saw him enter, she said, "Bruce, James, when I give the word, take your knee off and remove the towel. James, you pour vodka into the wound," Maggie tried to catch her breath.

"When that's done, get a clean towel over it. Bruce, use your knee to apply pressure like your father is now."

There was blood all over the bed sheets, all over their clothes, and it was dripping onto the floor.

Bruce said while crying, "Mom, there is blood everywhere. We have to get you to the hospital."

Maggie gasped, "No hospitals. Is everyone ready?... Now!"

James lifted his knee off Maggie's chest. Bruce removed the blood-soaked towel and handed the vodka to James. He poured about two shots of the clear antiseptic over the wound.

Maggie tried not to scream. The pain was so intense she let out a long and loud muffled grunting sound. James put a clean towel over her breasts, and Bruce applied the pressure with his knee over the towel.

Maggie was breathing fast and hard. "Agg hum! Agg hum! Give me some of the vodka to drink James."

James placed the bottle near her lips and Maggie took three large gulps. "Okay, I'm going to slow down my metabolism. That should help slow the bleeding. When I say now, take off the towel and James, you go into the wound with those tweezers. Find the bullet and pull it out."

"I can't Maggie," James was sweating badly. "I'm just a hack. I don't know what I'm doing. I can't do this."

Maggie said more calmly, "You aren't a hack, James. You got this. Stay with me you two. I will not die alone."

She took a few minutes to calm down even more. She used her mind to focus on her heartbeat. She made her heart slow down.

When she felt the time was right, she calmly said, "Now."

Bruce removed his knee and the towel. James took the tweezers and inserted them into the wound.

Maggie inhaled. "Hurry up James. This hurts like hell."

"I think I got it," James said, elated. Then quickly breathed out in frustration. "Damn! I lost it. It slipped out."

"Again, James and hurry. You pulled it closer to the exit."

James tried again. He found the bullet right away through all the gushing blood and gently pulled it out. He smiled as he stared at the red-soaked piece of lead.

"Yes!" shouted Bruce.

Maggie smiled a little. "Very good Doctor James Cannon. Now use the gauze from the kit, clean me up, and apply more pressure. I need to rest a bit."

James said, "Me too, and I need a few shots of that vodka."

Maggie said softly, "Not yet James. We are not done. We must all go through the procedures for the antidote. We were breathing hydrogen cyanide gas."

Sally was behind the front desk of The Hotel Excelsior, checking in some hotel guests. Hector called her on the phone.

His Spanish was eloquent. *"Have you seen James? He was here earlier. It is a busy day, and now he's gone."*

Sally answered, *"Oh, sorry Hector. Maggie called earlier. The three of them took a ride up north to Todos Santos. Maggie wanted to visit a hotel up there."*

"Why? We have a hotel here. A busy one that needs their help."

"Maggie never does anything with her family. This is a good sign. I guess she likes The Eagles."

"Why would they drive up there to see some birds? We have birds here in Los Cabos."

Sally tried to explain, *"No Hector. The Eagles are an American rock band. Rumor has it that the hotel in Todos Santos inspired them to write the famous song 'Hotel California'."*

"Why don't they write a song about our hotel? It is better than anything they have in Todos Santos. Just give me my mariachis. To hell with rock and roll."

"This is all good Hector. Maybe she will stay longer this time. Maggie said she wanted to do some serious family bonding."

Bruce pulled the three antidote kits out from under the bed. He put them on the bed and opened them. "What is this stuff?" he asked.

Maggie lay in the center of their king bed. Bruce was sitting on the bed to her left and James on her right. They were all wearing gas masks. The kit was a small white plastic box that contained some tablets, two bottles of medicine, gauze pads, two IV needles connected to six inches of thin plastic hose, and each kit had a stopwatch.

Maggie started coughing before she spoke, "I think the bleeding has stopped. Let's start the treatment." She coughed some more. "James, you need to help me. I should go first. I got the most gas."

James said, "What the hell do we do with this stuff?"

Maggie explained, "First, we do the amyl nitrite. That's the tablets. Break them up into pieces on the gauze pad. Open the mask slightly. Hold it under your nose for thirty seconds, then take it away and close the mask for thirty seconds. Use the stopwatch. We do this four times."

James broke up the tablet and Maggie opened her mask as James put it under her nose. Bruce and James did the same with the other two tablets.

"This stuff smells raunchy, like dirty socks," Bruce said with a disgusting look through the mask.

"Just do it Bruce," Maggie ordered.

When the first task was complete Maggie continued her antidote lesson. "We are not going to take any chances. Take the bottle marked sodium nitrite. Connect it to the hose end of the IV. Clean the needle of the IV and the insertion point with the antiseptic wipe."

"What's an insertion point?" Bruce asked.

"That's where you are going to stick the needle into your vein."

Bruce complained, "I can't do that. Stick myself with a needle, no way."

"Just do it Bruce," James demanded.

"Help me, James. I'm a little under the weather," Maggie asked.

James found a vein on Maggie's wrist. He cleaned the needle and her wrist with an antiseptic pad and gently inserted it into Maggie's vein.

"Now tape it on. Once the medicine is going in, start your stopwatch. We are going for seven minutes."

When time was up Maggie said, "Now take it out and rip off the tape."

James and Bruce did so with the tape painfully ripping off some arm hair.

James asked Maggie, "You have everything so well planned. Why didn't you just tell us what was going on? You put us at risk."

"Yeah, Mom, and we have four dead guys out there," Bruce added.

Maggie answered, "I have my reasons. We must continue. One more step. Now take the bottle marked sodium thiosulfate. Connect it to the other IV, then clean it and insert it. This time we go for fifteen minutes."

While they let the medicine flow into their bodies, James said, "Yes, Maggie, we have four dead guys out there. What are we going to do?"

"Why the third degree? Don't you remember I just got shot? I have some good men coming here tonight after one in the morning. They will discreetly take the bodies away. They will never be seen again."

"Do they dump them into Divorce Beach?" James asked.

Maggie said, "I don't ask. Okay time's up. Bruce, go out there and open the windows with the keypad and keep the curtains shut. Do not open the door and keep the masks on. I have a meter out there that will tell us when it is safe to remove them."

As Bruce left the room, James said again through the mask, "Why didn't you tell me what was going on?"

"James, please do me a favor?"

"That doesn't answer my question. What favor?"

Maggie smiled through the pain in her chest. "I want you to come to Paris with me for a nice romantic getaway."

"Wait a minute, Maggie. These guys were French. Something tells me this will be anything but a romantic getaway."

⁂

A nervous Louis Dubois waited impatiently for his son Frédéric to show up. The eighty-year-old bald man was not happy. Even the grand amenities of his large office did nothing to cheer him up. His office was filled with mahogany wood trim and lush indoor plants. He had a three-hole putting green to the left of his desk and a pool table to the right. The bar behind his desk would automatically open to reveal a six-person bubbling hot tub with a trickling six-foot waterfall filling the office with warmth. He pushed a button to unlock the office door when he heard a knock.

The skinny half-nerd Frédéric Dubois entered the office and sat down in a comfy chair in front of the patriarch of the Dubois family. *"Any word yet, Father?"*

The old man spoke harshly, *"Nothing. It has been two weeks now with no word from them. Your brother and cousin vanished into thin air along with two other good men."*

"I told you not to send them. They were sitting ducks for Maggie Love."

Louis Dubois stood up and yelled, *"Shut up Frédéric! They will turn up. There is no way that one woman took out four of our best. You should concentrate on helping us find them."*

Frédéric said timidly, *"What happened to the two men you sent to Mexico to try to find them?"*

"Dead. There is a police report on them. Looks like they got into it with some Mexican gang members. Both were shot."

"No doubt Maggie Love had something to do with that."

Louis yelled again, *"Shut up Frédéric! You are supposed to be the smart one. That's why I sent you to a top American university. Find them or you are going to Mexico."*

"Please father. Don't send me to Mexico. Maggie Love is a witch. She will kill me. I guess it doesn't matter where we are. If she has to, Maggie Love will kill us here in France."

Louis tried to calm down. *"So how is this Maggie Love going to break in here and kill us?"*

"I don't know father. I told you that she is a witch. She might put a spell on the guards, then come in here and kill us with knives or guns. She easily got past the guard and killed Uncle Paul. We may get the same fate as Alexander and Richard got."

"And what is that?" Louis asked.

Frédéric started to get hysterical. *"I do not know. I do know they are dead, and we are next. Maggie Love is going to kill us. I'm getting the hell out of here!"*

Louis tried to calm his son down. *"Settle down Frédéric, I need you strong. I will post extra guards around the house, and you can move in here for a while. Bring your wife and little boy. You will be safe here and, if this woman does try anything, we will kill her. I will make sure Maggie Love dies a slow horrible death."*

⁓

Their first-class seats were soft and fully reclined. They had already survived a flight from Cabo to Los Angeles. Now they were on a nonstop flight to Paris, France. Maggie and James could not sleep on airplanes. They were both watching the same movie *The Blind Side* on the screen in front of them. James tried to hold Maggie's hand.

Maggie took off her headset. "You know James, I have a few things to do when we get to Paris."

"So much for our romantic getaway. Are we going to see anything or do anything?"

"Sure, but I am going to be pretty busy. I might even need your help."

"I'm afraid to ask. Maggie Love never needs help, so what can I do?"

"Not much. I'll tell you when we get there. You are what I'm calling Plan C."

Maggie looked out the window of the 747 aircraft. She could see all the lights of the east coast abruptly end. They were over the Atlantic Ocean now. Seven more hours of flight and they would land in the Paris morning dew.

The couple got into a van going to the long-term parking lot. The drive took them through the hassle and hustle of Charles de Gaulle Airport. The lot was about ten kilometers away, and Maggie remembered exactly where she parked her car over nine months ago.

"What hotel are we staying at?" James asked as they got onto the green Volkswagen Bug.

"We're not staying in a hotel. I have a place here in Paris. I come here quite often," Maggie replied.

"You come here quite often, and this is the first time you ever asked me to come?"

"James, I told you, I have things to do here. I'm always terribly busy."

Maggie drove the forty-minute drive from the airport to Paris. The morning sky was clear of rain. This October day in 2009 was cool and partly cloudy. The traffic was brisk.

"You should have learned to speak French James. It comes in handy here."

James replied, "I had enough trouble picking up Spanish."

"And James, you saw my passport. My name is Tommie Scott while we are here."

"I know that. Can I have an alias too?"

"It would be tough to get the forged documents now but not impossible. Who do you want to be?"

"I was thinking about James Bond. That way you would only have to change one name."

Maggie laughed, "James Cannon sounds just as cool as James Bond, even cooler."

※

"I'm parking in a garage. I like these little cars in the tiny streets of Paris. It's still almost impossible to find a place to park near the condo."

Maggie turned right off the Rue Des Halles into an underground entrance. She opened the gate blocking the entrance of the lot with a key card and the gate opened. She drove a winding path down two levels until she got to her spot. The two got out and James unloaded their two carry-on suitcases from the back seat.

Maggie said, "I rented these two parking places for one month. Very expensive in this area."

"Why do we need two places?"

"One is for your car, James."

"Oh yeah," James said sarcastically. "I'm plan C. It would be nice to know what plans A and B are."

"James, I am going to have to tell you some day."

"Sure. At least I know we are going to be here a month. Do you think Sally, Hector and Bruce are going to be okay at the hotel for a whole month without us?"

"They will be fine. I told them to hire a good manager to replace you, and I am never there anyway. It might be less than a month. Either way, I am going to be remarkably busy."

They found an elevator and rode it up to the ground level. A short walk took them to the streets of Paris. A bustling French café with outdoor tables on their left and small businesses of every kind lined both sides of the street. Above the businesses were three stories of old, golden architecture, three stories of windows filled with lofts and apartments. Each window had at least a hundred years of stories to tell.

Maggie told James, "My apartment is about a five-minute walk north, but let's go left here. After all that flying, I want you to walk me through the park."

The park was called the *Jardin des Halles*. It was located above the gigantic underground shopping complex called The Halles Forum. About a hundred and seventy insanely busy shops, restaurants, and movie theaters thrived below them. Above, the park was modern and filled with lush green full-bodied trees and layered beds of colorful flowers. The paths they walked through were white and wide. The green grass around them was scattered with small groups of sitting Parisians and tourists. Numerous odd-shaped statues and sculptures were placed all around in the perfect spots.

James took Maggie's hand. "At least I get to see something. It's beautiful here."

"This might be it with me. I'm going to be oh-so busy," Maggie answered.

"We have to go see the Eiffel Tower, Maggie."

"Why is it that all tourists are so fascinated with the Eiffel Tower? It's always so crowded, and you've seen tons of pictures."

"I just want to see it. Can I ask you one favor while we are here?"

"What is it, James?"

"Never mind. It is a silly request. I thought you might…"

They walked out of the park and went east on the Rue Rambuteau. This street was again lined with shops sitting below majestic apartments and lofts. They stopped when they got to a tall blue door, cut in-between a pasta restaurant and a women's clothing store.

"This is it." Maggie opened the door with a large blue key.

Inside was a small open-aired atrium filled with green plants and shrubs. They walked to the elevator, pushed their wheeled suitcases inside, and rode it to the third floor.

Maggie's condo was modernly decorated with a good amount of French flare. Paintings on the walls were colored with soft browns and oranges that matched the brown leather couches and chairs. There was a strange display of a blue-handled Japanese katana sword in a polished green and blue case.

"This is nice, Maggie. A little over decorated for your taste, no?"

"I did the swords. The rest was here when I bought it."

"Thought so," James navigated the condo. "We have a full kitchen, a living area, and a bedroom with a king bed. What's behind this door?"

Maggie said with force, "That's my place. You are not allowed in there."

"What am I, five years old?" James smiled. "Is that Mommy's secret woman's cave?"

"Okay, I'll show you. But when you want to come in, you have to knock."

Maggie opened the door. Inside were wooden tables and chairs with electric meters, batteries of every size, test tubes and beakers, tools, bunches of wires and three computers.

James said in a Dracula kind of voice, "Is this your se-car-ret la-bra-ra-tory, Doctor Frankenstein?"

"Yes, it is, and if you keep up that stupid voice, you will never be allowed in here again."

※

Maggie spent most days locked inside her workshop. James could hear her talking on her cell phone in French occasionally. Sometimes at night, she would leave, only to come back in the wee morning hours. At least three times a week an Asian man would knock on the door. With him would be bags filled with containers of Chinese food.

Maggie ran out of the workshop when he arrived. "Hello Mr. Chen."

Chen spoke in broken English, "Yes, Miss Scott, your food is ready and hot."

Maggie handed him a bunch of euros. "Thank you, Mr. Chen. Your food is the best in the city."

James spent his days looking at French TV or walking through the streets of Paris alone. He did walk the eight kilometers to the Eiffel Tower. It was an overcast day with the top of the 324-meter steeple disappearing into the clouds. There was a long line of people, hundreds long, waiting to get to the top.

James thought, "That is way too high up for me. I'm keeping my feet on the ground. Maggie was right; it is way too crowded here."

Maggie got home in the early morning. The sun had just come up. Maggie found a parking spot right next to the door of the condo, which was fortunate. She opened the front trunk and took out a large gunny sack. She threw it over her shoulder and walked towards the big blue door.

When she got inside the condo she called out to James, "Get up! I need to talk to you."

James slept in most days. He was surprised Maggie wanted to talk.

In the workshop, Maggie poured the contents of the sack onto a wooden table.

"What is this stuff, tasers?" James asked.

"Yes James, I am studying the batteries, the trigger, and the electrode projectile. There is more." She took one of two small leather cases. She opened it. Inside was a 38 special Smith and Wesson revolver. "This is my gun of choice, and I got you one just like it. If you prefer something else, I can exchange it."

"Maggie you must know that I have never shot a gun in my life."

"You know James, guns are not that hard to get in France, just a lot of paperwork. You bought them."

"I bought them. I don't even know how to shoot."

"You will learn James; you joined a club."

"What club?"

"A shooting club. They have a very nice range here, and I need to brush up on my shooting also. And you now have that alias you wanted."

"I was just kidding, Maggie. It's not James Bond, is it?"

"No silly. It's way cooler than that. You are now Gus Power."

She was tall and elegant. Her long, black hair hung loosely below her soft shoulders. She entered the mansion and strolled quickly across the foyer of the house like it was a runway at a fashion show. She climbed up the central spiral staircase then strode purposefully through the hall. She stopped at the last room on the right and opened the door. There she saw her husband Frédéric Dubois sitting behind a computer and her six-year-old son Clement staring at a big screen TV.

The former French fashion model, Eloise Dubois, stared down the room with fire coming out of her beautiful eyes. Her French was hotter than the fire in her eyes. *"Clement, get out of here. Go downstairs and play. I need to talk to your father."*

Little Clement scuffled out of the room and Eloise turned towards Frédéric. *"We have been here for weeks Frédéric. I didn't give up my career as a model and marry you to live with your parents."*

Frédéric sounded a little frightened. *"I'm so sorry my dear. I told you this is just temporary."*

"Shut up you little mouse, and why do we have to live in that little stinking apartment? Why can't we have a place like this without your parents?"

"I'm working on that, and I just need more time. It is safe here for now. We have some threats against the family."

Eloise got angrier. "You are such a coward. Be a man and defend your woman. Who is this scary man making these threats?"

"It is a witch named Maggie Love."

"What? It is a woman you are so scared of?"

"Yes, I believe she has killed several members of our family already."

Eloise got the last word in. "I'm getting out of this house. You are worse than a mouse; you are like a worm. You better keep sending me my allowance checks," she opened the door, "or you will never see your son again."

As she stormed out of the house, Frédéric put his head down on the keyboard of his computer and started to whimper, *"Maggie Love is coming. She is coming to kill us all."*

⌘

James could not figure it out. He would check his pockets in the morning, and they were always empty. When he went out for his afternoon walk, there would be euros, sticky notes and coins in his pockets. He even found a one-hundred euro note stuffed in his underwear. He decided to confront Maggie about this. He knocked on the workshop door.

"Come in, James," Maggie said from the other side of the door.

Maggie was sitting behind her desk staring at a computer screen. On one of the benches nearby were stacks of grey flat disks eight inches in diameter. James noticed them right away, "What's with all the mini-Frisbees?"

Maggie answered, "There're just hot pads, James. I'm working on some new hot-pad technology. You never know when you might need a good hot pad."

"Okay, but that's not why I wanted to talk. Somebody, somebody probably named Maggie, keeps stuffing money into my pockets. Why?"

"Do you notice it when I put the money in?"

"No, I find it when I'm walking around."

"Good. I'm getting better at it. I'm practicing on you."

James got a little flustered. "Practicing what?"

"Sleight of hand. You know how Paris is known for having the best pickpockets in the world? I want to learn how they do it."

"But Maggie, they take things out of your pockets. You are putting stuff in them."

"So, I got it backwards? Darn. But as long as you are here, I need to scan your right index fingerprint."

"I would ask why, but I know you won't tell me."

Maggie smiled, "Of course I will tell you James. It's part of plan C."

She stood up and gave James a very slight hug. "Time for me to get back to work."

James closed the door and went to sit down on the couch. He felt something in his underwear. He reached inside his drawers and pulled out one of Maggie's hot pads.

The house had the look of an old castle. Two rocky towers rose above the three-story mansion. It was surrounded by five acres of green grass, lush juniper, and yew trees, and Maggie knew this was the house she was looking for. James pulled his small brown Renault Clio near the curb about two blocks away from the house.

Maggie looked through the midnight scene and closed her laptop. "That's the place, James," Maggie said from the passenger's seat. "I hacked into their security system. All the cameras on the west side of the place will be off for twenty-five minutes."

Maggie was dressed in black tights with a black-knitted cap covering her hair. Underneath the black tights she wore a full-bodied wet suit.

James asked, "Why only the west side?"

"Because that's where the electrical box is. I'll be back in less than ten."

Maggie disappeared into the darkness carrying a small toolbox and a flashlight. James waited for what seemed like seconds when Maggie suddenly got back into the car.

"Where did you come from? I didn't see you."

"You didn't see me because I didn't want you to see me. Let's go. I'm done here for tonight."

"Okay Maggie, I understand you want to wear black to stay hidden in the night but why the wet suit? You're not going swimming."

"I might need it in two days. I want to get used to wearing it. On Sunday, we are coming back."

XII. THE ANGEL • 12. In Her Fifties

Maggie got up early. At six in the morning, she shook James until he woke up.

"Come on James. We have to go to the range after breakfast and practice some more. Your shooting stinks."

A groggy James tried to say, "I'm a beginner. How can I ever be as good as…"

"You may have to be tomorrow night if it comes to plan C. Here it is James. I am going to tell you. Plan A: I go into the mansion and come out ten minutes later. We get the hell out of there in your car. Plan B: I go into the mansion. In ten minutes, all the lights go out. I come out two minutes later. We get the hell out in your car. Plan C: The lights go out. I do not come out in two minutes. You come in with your gun and flashlight to help me."

"Maggie, I have never shot anyone before."

"It's not going to come to that. Besides, if you can pull a bullet out of my chest, you can easily shoot a few Frenchmen."

James got up and looked out the window at the wonderful French fall morning. "Maggie, can I have a last request before we do this?"

"What is it James?"

"I want to walk through the park."

"Sure, we can walk through the park this afternoon."

"Maggie, I don't want to walk through the park with you."

Maggie said with surprise, "James! Don't tell me you already have a cute little French mistress."

"No, no it's not that, not that at all. I want to walk the park with Molly Jones, like you were when we first met."

"I didn't bring that wig. I guess we can find one around here somewhere. This is the fashion capital of the world." Maggie said with her most nasally voice, "Yes, yes James. Yes, you do have an afternoon date with Molly Jones."

☙❦❧

Maggie seemed out of place on this cool afternoon in the *Jardin de Halles*. The casually-dressed park visitors made Maggie seem even nerdier than she was. She wore a brown business suit with dark brown low-heeled shoes. Her dark brown La Belle Époque wig went perfectly with her oversized square thick-rimmed brown glasses.

James had a big smile on his face as they navigated through the park. He held out his arm with the hope that she would take it.

Maggie said nasally, "No, no James. No arm holding. Not my boyfriend, no, no."

James asked, "At least can we go get some Chinese and a glass of wine?"

"No, very bad, the wine. Only Chen can bring me Chinese. James, you must stop the hacking. Very bad the hacking."

"Maybe we can go to my place and watch *Dirty Dancing*. I got a big screen."

"No, no. No *Dirty Dancing*. Very bad show."

"Well then, what do you want to do?"

Maggie did everything she could to keep from laughing. "I like the kinky James. S&M is very fun. Yes, yes, I love the kinky, love to be the master."

"If we're playing S&M, I'm being the master and you are my nerdy slave girl."

The couple almost ran back to the condo. Both were overanxious for a round of really weird and crazy roleplay.

"Are you tired already, James? I want one more."

"Three is my limit, Maggie."

The exhausted James got out of bed and looked into the darkness outside the condo. The naked man turned to Maggie. "Why can't we just go back to Cabo? Why do we have to do this Maggie? We can have a good long life there."

"I can't do that. I have tried. I cannot let these people that ruined my parents' lives get away with it and live in the lap of luxury."

"Try a little harder. I'm not sure I can do this."

"You can go back to Cabo, James. You don't have to help me."

"I said I would do it, and I will. Now I'm starting to sound like you."

"That's good James. We can sleep in tomorrow morning. When 10:00 p.m. comes around, that's twenty-two hundred hours, I'm going into that house."

They were both wearing black tights, black-knitted caps, and black gloves. Maggie parked the Volkswagen a block from the mansion while James parked the Renault three blocks away.

XII. THE ANGEL • 12. In Her Fifties

Maggie ran back to his car and got in the passenger seat. She opened her laptop.

"This is it, James. I have access to all the cameras now, and it looks like the old man is in his room upstairs. The son and grandson are asleep in their room. There are only two guards sitting in a den playing cards downstairs. I'm going to turn off the all the cameras in the house, then in the back door I go."

"I'm scared to death Maggie. Tell me this is going to work."

Maggie felt something. A strange feeling stretching across her entire being. It made her gasp. "James, I just had an intense feeling of Déjà vu. Plan C will happen."

"Don't say that, Maggie. I can't do this."

"You can. When all the lights go out, only two things in the house will work. The fingerprinted keypad on the front door and the keypad on the office door. Your right index fingerprint will open them both. Remember to take your glove off. Take the stairs to the second floor. The office is the third door on the left. That is where I will be. Remember your flashlight and gun." Maggie opened the car door and disappeared into the darkness.

Big Jon had lost all his money. Slick Marvin beat him on the last hand of poker with a full house.

"Maybe you need to go to your Mommy's house and borrow some money. It's early yet." Slick Marvin's French sounded a little weaselly.

Big John was musty-haired and obese. At over three-hundred pounds, he was way larger than the slim and well-dressed Slick Marvin. They looked like a French version of Laurel and Hardy.

Big Jon said, *"Did you hear something? I can hear a pin drop, and I just heard a pin drop. Someone came in the back door."*

Maggie opened the back door with her fingerprint. She shined her flashlight on the floor and saw the pin. She faked like she was trying to get out. The door had relocked, and soon she was tackled to the floor by the thin Frenchman.

Big Jon turned on the kitchen light. Slick Marvin got Maggie back on her feet.

Jon said, *"So this is the scary woman that has Frédéric shitting his pants?"*

"She's a hot-looking broad. Let's get her upstairs and show the boss."

Maggie acted like she was angry. "You two assholes leave me alone. I've had enough of you French morons."

The two henchmen had trouble getting Maggie up the stairs. She was kicking and punching them all the way up. She repeated over and over, "Leave me alone, you fat piece of French lard." Little did they know the struggle was totally fake.

When they got to the top, Louis Dubois was in his bathrobe and waiting by his office door.

Slick Marvin said, "Look what we found Boss."

The patriarch said back, "Yes, good job boys. Take her into my office. Marvin, you go get Frédéric at once."

Louis went behind his desk and sat down while Big Jon held Maggie tightly.

"So, you are the infamous witch," Louis said dryly. "Where are my son and nephew, Maggie Love?"

Maggie answered angrily, "I don't know what you are talking about. You better let me go. This is kidnapping."

Slick Marvin and Frédéric soon entered the office. A shaky and rattled Frédéric said, "That's Maggie Love. Be careful Big Jon. She is a witch."

The bald and old Louis reached into a drawer of his desk. He took out a Glock 43 pistol. He put it on his desk.

"Take that Frédéric."

His son said back, "Don't make me shoot her. She is a witch. She will come back to life and kill me."

Louis said sternly to Frédéric, "Take the gun, coward. I do not want you to shoot her. Just cover her. That is too fast a death for Maggie Love. I have something slower planned. Did you boys frisk her?"

Big Jon said, "Yes boss, we frisked her good. Real nice body, but she is clean. Another thing. This dumb broad is wearing a wetsuit."

"A wetsuit?" Louis smiled. "That's perfect because our lovely guest is going for a swim."

He pushed a button behind his desk. The bar behind his desk opened and the bubbling hot tub was revealed. He turned on the six-foot waterfall for added ambience.

Frédéric took the gun and with shaking hands he pointed it at Maggie. Big Jon and Slick Marvin started to force Maggie towards the hot tub. Maggie did some more fake struggling and fake acting. She spoke in English, "Don't do it! Let me go." She continued to kick and squirm. She did not need to. She had already accomplished her task.

During the struggle up the stairs, Maggie managed to secretly place two of her hot pads into each of the henchmen's trousers. She didn't count on the water. She hoped her wetsuit would do its job.

Big Jon forced Maggie's head into the bubbling water. Maggie didn't try to bring her head up. Instead she went down deeper into the water.

Louise watched with delight as the two men tried to drown Maggie Love. Even the shaky Frédéric started to smile.

After two minutes, Maggie desperately needed air. She reached her fingers through a slit in the wetsuit. In a very private place, she had a small remote control hidden. She pushed the button twice, sending out two signals.

The first signal set off the four hot pads in the henchmen's pants, delivering fifty thousand volts of electricity into each man. The water conducted the electricity even more effectively. The men screamed loudly as the electric current burned through their bodies. The wetsuit insulated Maggie, and she didn't feel a thing. When she felt the man release her, she dove her body under the water and swam to the other side of the tub. She got her head above water and took a deep breath. It was pitch black. The second signal shut off all the power in the entire house.

"*I'm over here,*" Maggie said into the darkness.

⚜

James Cannon saw the lights go out in the house. He didn't wait the two minutes. He got out of the car and jogged the three blocks to the front door of the place. He took off his right glove and placed his shaking finger on the sensor of the keypad. The door opened. Then he heard a gunshot.

⚜

Louis Dubois was frantic. He kept repeating loudly, "*Shoot her! Shoot her, Frédéric!*"

An almost crying Frédéric, said, "*I can't see her. She is invisible. She is a witch.*" He fired once at Maggie's voice, missing her by a mile.

Maggie made her way behind the pool table. She crouched below it, then suddenly stood up. *"I'm over here. I'm over here."*

He fired two more shots at the voice. Both were wild misses.

Louis continued to yell, *"Where are the guards! Where are the guards!"*

The sobbing Frédéric said, *"They got shocked to death. She put an evil spell on them."*

Maggie snuck low and crawled toward the old man's desk. She got behind him and said, *"I'm over here. I'm over here."*

She quickly moved to her right. Another shot and she heard a slight bump. She could barely make out the old man's head slumped down on his desk.

James ran up the spiral staircase. He had now heard five gunshots. When he got to his room of choice, he again used his fingerprint to open the door. He shined his light inside and saw a little man with glasses holding a gun. The man slowly turned towards him. James fired his gun once, and the man fell to the floor.

Maggie was now by his side. "It's almost over James. Give me the flashlight."

Maggie turned Frédéric's body over, so they could see his face. Maggie said in her southern accent, "That's some pretty dandy shootin' there, Tex. You got him right between them eyes."

"I was aiming for his chest," James dropped the gun. "Maggie I just killed a man."

Maggie took the gun and flashlight and went over to check the bodies of the guards. Then she went to the desk of Louis Dubois. "Damn it James, he's dead."

"I thought that's what you wanted?"

"I did, but I wanted to do it. I guess it is a little ironic how I was forced to kill my own mother, and now Frédéric kills his own father,"

"The biggest difference is that he's dead, and you are not."

"Right James. We have to get the hell out of here."

The couple left the office and locked the door. In the dark hall they came across a little boy wandering around in his pajamas.

"Don't kill him, Maggie."

Maggie crouched down to the little boy, "James, shine the light on my face." Then she spoke in slow French, *"What is your name little boy"*

"My name is Clement Dubois. All the lights went off, and I'm scared."

"Listen Clement, my name is Mademoiselle Amor. I want you to be a good boy. If I ever find out that you start being bad. I will come and find you. Let's go James."

They rushed out of the house and ran towards James's car. When they got close to the Volkswagen, James said, "Maggie there is somebody in your car."

"No there's not. Just get to your car."

They got into the Renault. Maggie immediately started typing into her laptop. "James they are almost here."

James started the car. "Then we should get out of here."

"Not yet." Maggie took a small remote control out of the glovebox.

Soon a big black Cadillac pulled up behind the Volkswagen. Three large men got out and approached the little car. One of them had a crowbar. He started breaking the windows.

"Now." Maggie pushed the button on the remote. The explosion was loud, violent and filled with yellow, orange, and red fire. The fire grew larger, engulfing the three men in flames.

Their screams could easily be heard three blocks away.

"Now James. Let's go."

James sped the car away as fast as it could go. "What the hell just happened?"

Maggie smiled. "It's amazing what you can do with a few good hot pads."

"We are going to be on this damn train for twelve hours?"

"Yes James. I promised you a romantic getaway, and that's exactly what you're getting. Just not in Paris. Vienna is just as nice."

"Maggie who were those men in the Cadillac that you blew up?"

The train was speeding through the middle of Europe at a relaxing speed. Their first-class seats were comfy and warm.

"They were from a rival clan of the Dubois, the Peltier clan. I kind of stole some money from them."

"Why were they there?"

Maggie said softly, "Because I wanted them there. I let them find out that I gave the money to the Dubois's. I even let them know what time I would be there and what kind of car I had. The manikin in the car did resemble me a bit."

"Why did you do all this?" James asked.

"The authorities are going to think this whole thing was a gang war between the Dubois and the Peltier clans."

James said, "You figured it all out. Hey, somebody's smoking on this train. I thought that wasn't allowed."

Maggie looked over her shoulder. She saw the smoking man in the back. She turned to James. "You know I do love you, James. After all that has happened, I have loved you since our first date. What's amazing is, after all the things I have done, you still love me back." Maggie got up and scooted in front of James's seat, "I have to see someone in the back."

When she approached Inspector Lawrence, he said to her, "Did I just hear you say that you love James?"

"Sure, Lawrence. I can love. I'm not a heartless monster, you know." Maggie looked a little emotional.

"So, whatever happened to 'I can never feel love. It is impossible for me to feel love, because I am Love?'"

Maggie's eyes were starting to fill with tears. "That's just a silly riddle I wrote for James, years ago."

The Inspector stared at Maggie. "So, you really feel love?"

"Of course, Lawrence, I love James. I love Bruce. I love my parents. I even love the mother I shot."

"Not quite a repentance, but it's something." The Inspector looked a little relieved.

Maggie was trying her best not to cry. She changed the subject. "Yah, yah, what the hell do you want anyway?"

"I have news, Maggie. The Consul has made their decision about you."

Maggie said back with vigor, "So I'm being terminated. Who cares? I just killed seven people. My Guardian Angel gets to kill me now."

The Angel put out his cigarette on the floor. "No, I don't do that, and you have killed six. Now you have James killing."

"Are you on my side now? When does this termination happen?"

"I didn't say you were being terminated; I just said a decision has been made. I do not know what the decision is. The Consul wants to see one last thing."

"What the hell for? Just terminate me already. What more is there?"

"I'm sorry Maggie. I have my orders."

Maggie's mind exploded.

13. In Her Nineties

MAGGIE WOKE UP.

The room was dimly lit. It was cold, dark, and it smelled of death. There was no spinning or wind, just almost pitch darkness. Maggie's eyes were almost blind from cataracts and her once vibrant green eyes were now a pale grey. Her hair was white and unkept, and Maggie was now very thin and frail. She weighed a mere one-hundred-and-ten pounds. The room was dark because the light hurt her eyes and she did not want to see what she had become. Her bones were brittle and full of osteoporosis. There was a constant pain in her head because a cancer was destroying her once beautiful mind.

She lay in her bed waiting, soaking in all the loneliness around her. She had outlived all the people she knew. Her life partner, James, her son Bruce, and her mother and sister were all gone. Maggie wanted to live just one more day. Tomorrow was her birthday. It would be January 23, 2056, and tomorrow she would become a centurion.

Even with body and brain so crippled, she felt the *déjà vu* running through her. She felt she would die alone for the second time. She tried to reach for a glass of water on a nightstand by her bed. Her frail body slid off the bed with her head banging the nightstand as she fell to the floor. Maggie did not go under into the world of unconsciousness. Not for an instance did she think, "I have fallen, and I can't get up." She used the power of her mind to temporarily block the pain that was consuming her body and brain. Her thin arms mustered up the strength to pull her body up and back into her bed. She drank from her glass of water and again waited for her grim time to come.

Suddenly there was a presence of a man sitting on her bed next to her. He took her wrinkly hand in his.

Maggie said in a soft trembling tone, "Inspector Lawrence, can I live one more day? Just one more day is all. Then I will be one hundred years old. Stay with me please. You're my angel. I do not want to die alone."

"I don't think you are going to make it to one-hundred, Maggie. I cannot stay with you."

"It is torture to make a person die alone twice. That is worse than all the other tortures you put me through. I still will not repent. Terminate me now."

"Maggie, I don't know what the Consul's decision is yet. I cannot stay with you, but I made arrangements. I cashed in some favors, and I hope I can pull this off."

Suddenly the Inspector was gone. He disappeared into the darkness and Maggie was alone once again. She waited for her time when her soul would leave her body.

Her front door opened, and a bright light came in from around a dark silhouette. It was the silhouette of an African American man. He wore a long black trench coat with a matching black fedora. He closed the door and slowly approached Maggie. He knelt next to her bed.

"James?" Maggie asked. "You are so young."

"Yes Maggie. Lawrence is training me to be an Inspector. I chose to be in my thirties. That was my age when I first met you."

"It is not fair. You look so wonderful, young, and strong, and I'm so old and ugly."

He took her hands in his. "Maggie, you look as beautiful today as you did when I first saw you. You do not have to die alone. Inspector Lawrence somehow arranged this visit. I always and only wanted to be with you. Now, I can be with you until the end."

Maggie said clearly, with remorse in her voice, "James, I am so sorry I put you through all of that. You even killed for me. Such a good man you are. You deserved better than me."

James hugged her softly. "I wouldn't change a thing, Maggie. My life was perfect because I met the amazing Maggie Love."

Maggie tried to smile then she felt something break inside her head, like someone pulled out a plug. She slowly closed her eyes and let her soul leave her body. The last thing she heard in this world was James softly crying.

XIII. THE ANGEL

I FINALLY MADE IT BACK TO THE BLISS. THIS HAS ALWAYS BEEN A VERY happy place, but it seems a little different now. It was a little more serene and even more joyful than I ever remembered. There was a feeling of total contentment. When I looked up at the orbiting Consul, the three female Beings on top were moving in a clockwise circle. Quickly at first, then slowing down at the twelve o'clock. They kept repeating this motion over and over, three glorious lights swinging in the sky. Were they dancing? Soon the two male Beings joined in. I knew why. It is incredible what a little bit of love can do, and there was so much of it everywhere. I was sure Maggie Love would not be terminated.

I soon met with the Consul, and I immediately resigned my Inspectorship. Younger souls can do a much better job as an Inspecting Angel than I can. So what do these Consulers do? They give me another assignment. A much more difficult assignment. I have told you this before. What we have known for thousands of years here in the Bliss, you still don't get it on the Below World.

The Female soul is superior to the Male soul. They want me to form a task force that can somehow prove this to the people of The Below World.

The Consul has instructed me to pick a strong, intelligent female to direct this operation. They suggested I should use some of the famous and accomplished Female Beings from our past history. They recommended leaders like Margret Thatcher, Cleopatra, or Joan of Arc. Fine leaders they are, and there are many more.

But if I must do this, I am going to do it my way. I know this might sound ridiculous to some, but I do not care. To me, this makes total sense. And I know that most of you that have read this journal have to agree.

I am choosing Maggie Love.

About the Author

C. R. FABIS is a retired dessert chef who invented thousands of desserts for major chains, high-end restaurants, and fast-food joints. He is a cartoonist with thousands of followers on Instagram and loves to write novels that are hard to classify. He lives in Littleton, Colorado with his wife, 4 cats, and 1 dog.

www.ingramcontent.com/pod-product-compliance
Lightning Source LLC
LaVergne TN
LVHW010307070426
835512LV00029B/3496